Wildflowers
of
Glacier National Park
and Surrounding Areas

Also by Peter Lesica
with illustrations by Debbie McNeil

A Flora of Glacier National Park

Available from
Oregon State University Press

Wildflowers
of
Glacier National Park
and Surrounding Areas

Marias Pass

by
Shannon Fitzpatrick Kimball
and
Peter Lesica

TRILLIUM
P·R·E·S·S

© 2005 by Trillium Press, Kalispell, Montana.

Distributed by Riverbend Publishing, Helena, Montana.
Printed in South Korea
The Cataloging-in-Publication data is on file at Library of Congress.
ISBN 1-931832-54-5

All photographs, including cover (Mount Clements), by Peter Lesica.

DISCLAIMER: Consuming and/or using plants for medicinal purposes is extremely dangerous and my result in death or serious injury. The authors, publishers and distributors of this book do not recommend experimentation with edible and medicinal plants by readers.

CONTENTS

DEDICATIONS

For John and Carolyn.
S.K.

For Mary Caroline, who is a better photographer
but doesn't have as much film.
P.L.

ACKNOWLEDGMENTS

Many thanks to a handful of people who helped the authors as this book was created. Technical guidance from Chris Cauble and Brad Lamson and editorial help from Beth Judy and D.D. Dowden were critical to the success of this project. We also appreciate the work of Andy Cagle and Richard Menicke in providing the map.

Thank you to Jen Asebrook, Jerry DeSanto and Jack and Rachel Potter for the time spent hiking together and their shared interest in Glacier's flora. They made invaluable contributions to this book over the past several years by sharing their knowledge of the park and its ecology.

Shannon wishes to recognize the unending support of family and friends. Thank you to John Kimball, Carol McKeever-Hawes, Ralph Fitzpatrick, Quinn Fitzpatrick, Dick Hawes, Brad Lamson, Jen Asebrook, Jenny Tollefson, Sonja Hartmann, Lisa McKeon, Kelly Davidson, Terry Divoky, Angie Evenden, and Pam Robinson for your interest and friendship. And thank you, Carolyn, for your patience while Mom worked on her book.

INTRODUCTION

Glacier National Park is one of the most breathtaking natural areas in North America. With its jagged peaks, shimmering lakes and lush valleys, Glacier's scenery leaves visitors awestruck at every turn. In addition, native plant communities flourish relatively untouched by human activity, allowing amateur and professional naturalists the opportunity to study and enjoy.

Glacier National Park was established in 1910 by an act of Congress. The park encompasses roughly 4,000 square kilometers (about a million acres) and is bordered by Canada's Waterton Lakes National Park to the north. Glacier National Park lies immediately north of the Bob Marshall Wilderness Complex, an extensive, protected wilderness area with rugged, mountainous terrain. The mountains within Glacier National Park lie along the main range of the Rocky Mountains, with many peaks rising 8,000–10,000 feet (2,450–3,050 meters). The Continental Divide winds its way from northwest to southeast along the tallest peaks, separating the upper reaches of streams that flow into the Pacific and Atlantic oceans. A portion of a second divide, the Northern Divide, meanders through the eastern side of Glacier National Park, separating the Arctic and Atlantic oceans.

Climate

Within Glacier National Park, two distinctly different weather patterns dictate the climates east and west of the Continental Divide. Warm, moist air moves from the Pacific Ocean, following the jet stream in an easterly direction. As it approaches the Continental Divide, the air cools and moisture is lost in the form of precipitation. There-

Hole-in-the-Wall

fore, the western side of the park receives significantly more rain and snow than the eastern side. East of the Continental Divide, the climate is heavily influenced by cold arctic air masses pressing south from Canada. The high peaks of the Continental Divide confine this cold air to the eastern side of the park, with some spilling over and draining into the western high country. The resulting climate is markedly drier and colder than that west of the Continental Divide. Near the Continental Divide, this difference becomes much less apparent, since the alpine environments on both sides of the divide are subject to similar weather patterns.

Geology

The rugged mountains, steep slopes, narrow valleys and amphitheater-like cirque headwalls that characterize Glacier National Park are geologic formations produced by the action of ice and water on up-lifted sedimentary (primarily) and igneous rock. Most of the sedimentary formations within the park were deposited in what was once a shallow sea, 800 million to over a billion years ago in the Precambrian age. The deposits were folded and lifted 65–70 million years ago along an overthrust zone, creating a long band of solid rock running roughly northwest to southeast. This rock was carved by the repeated advance and retreat of glaciers that covered the area during the last ice age. Today only about forty glaciers in the park continue to carve and reshape rock on a small scale. These glaciers are getting smaller, the result of a warming trend that is affecting most of our planet.

The combined effect of climate and geology has produced a vast array of habitats suitable for plant growth. High-elevation plant communities have adapted to the bitter wind, lack of soil

Logan Pass

and short growing season. Many coniferous forests on the western side of the park have a warm coastal character, while forests on the eastern side are drier and more open. Valley bottomlands are home to riparian stream corridors, wetlands, meadows and grasslands with unique and interesting native plants. Examination of these habitats and the plants that occupy them is a fascinating activity, providing an interesting view of the roles climate and geology have played in shaping Glacier National Park into the natural wonder it is today.

Vegetation Zones

Elevation has a powerful impact on the development of vegetation. With increased elevation there is a decrease in temperature and an increase in wind and precipitation. These environmental factors are sometimes moderated in rugged, mountainous terrain. In Glacier National Park, elevation can be used to define three different vegetation zones. These zones and corresponding elevation ranges are:

Zone	Elevation Range
Montane	3,000–5,500 ft (915–1,675 m)
Subalpine	5,000–7,500 ft (1,525–2,285 m)
Alpine	>6,500 ft (>1,980 m)

The following is merely a summary of these three vegetation zones and the complex plant communities they support. A more detailed description of plant communities in all three zones is available in *A Flora of Glacier National Park* (Lesica 2002).

Montane Zone

The mild climate of the montane zone permits the development of a wide range of plant communities. In Glacier National Park, this zone is made up of grasslands, wetlands and three distinct types of forests: riparian, aspen and coniferous. Glacier's mon-

Big Prairie

tane **grasslands** are primarily located near the eastern and western boundaries of the park. Native grasslands are dominated by tussock-forming native grasses, such as rough fescue and bluebunch wheatgrass. **Wetlands** include wet meadows, swamps, marshes and fens, often associated with aquatic features such as streams, lakes and beaver ponds. While not extensive, these areas support some of the park's most fascinating and rare plant species. **Riparian forests** develop on the floodplains of rivers and large streams. New riparian forests are constantly regenerating as these waterways meander from one channel to another. **Aspen forests** are primarily found on the eastern side of Glacier National Park, near the eastern boundary. These deciduous forests often develop adjacent to grasslands and may cover extensive areas. The undergrowth in aspen forests is lush due to the penetration of light in early spring.

Montane **coniferous forests** cover mountain slopes and benches with many different forest types. West of the divide, lush, wet forests lie in the McDonald Valley, while drier forests occur along the western edge of the park. Because the eastern climate is more extreme, montane coniferous forests are uncommon on the eastern side of the park. Coniferous forests east of the divide are more typical of the subalpine zone; these forest types extend to lower elevations.

Waterton Valley

McDonald Valley

Subalpine Zone

The subalpine zone supports four main vegetation types: grasslands, meadows, avalanche chutes and coniferous forests. Subalpine **grasslands** are similar in plant composition to montane grasslands, although hardier species become more common at higher elevations. These grasslands often develop on south- and west-facing slopes and in areas where exposure to wind prohibits the establishment of other plants. Two different types of **meadows** common in the subalpine zone are dominated by broad-leaved herbaceous plants and sedges. Wet meadows, common around the Logan Pass Visitor Center, occur on level or gentle terrain in areas where snow accumulates. Dry meadows may develop on steep, rocky slopes where plant cover is sparse due to frequent downhill movement of soil. Dry meadows carpeted with beargrass often form on slopes with a more moderate grade. Beargrass meadows frequently develop into open subalpine forests as trees establish over time. **Avalanche chutes** filled with tall, flexible shrubs are common in steep ravines where snow slides downhill in the spring. Avalanche chutes are visible on high mountain slopes along Going-to-the Sun Road. Vast tracts of **coniferous forest** blanket mountain slopes throughout the subalpine zone of Glacier National Park. Most subalpine forests are dominated by subalpine fir and Engelmann spruce, but Douglas fir, lodgepole

Dry Fork of the Two Medicine River

Preston Park

pine and western larch are also abundant. Higher subalpine forests subject to severe wind and snow accumulation often develop a stunted growth form called krummholz.

Alpine Zone

The harsh alpine climate severely limits plant growth in this vegetation zone, resulting in the formation of low-growing, sparsely vegetated plant communities. Alpine vegetation can be loosely grouped into four different types: fellfields, turf, snow fields and talus/scree. **Fellfields** cover significant portions of the alpine landscape in Glacier National Park. These areas are dominated by alpine dryad, which forms stripes of vegetation perpendicular to the slope. Alpine **turf** communities develop in more protected sites. Turf vegetation is typically dense, though plants rarely grow more than 5 inches high. Areas where snow persists late in the summer often form **snow field** vegetation. This plant community, dominated by dwarf shrubs and sedges, is a relatively minor vegetation type in the park. Vegetation that develops on **talus and scree** is subject to constant shifting due to the steepness of these slopes. A wide variety of alpine plants including Jacob's ladder and silky phacelia are sparsely distributed among the rock on talus and scree slopes.

Gable Pass

Fire

Wildfire has a tremendous impact on the structure and composition of forested areas throughout Glacier National Park in all vegetation zones. Burned montane and subalpine forests of subalpine fir and Engelmann spruce give way to monocultures of lodgepole pine, a tree that establishes abundantly after severe fire. Over time these forests return to subalpine fir and Engelmann spruce as the lodgepole age and become vulnerable to insects and disease. The understory also changes dramatically. Species like fireweed flourish after fire clears the area of competing vegetation. Gradually other perennial shrubs and herbaceous species establish, some sprouting from surviving roots and some from seed sources in the forest soil or neighboring areas. Ponderosa pine trees, with their thick, fire-resistant bark, may survive low- to moderate-intensity wildfire that clears away understory shrubs and competing conifers. In these situations, open, park-like stands of mature ponderosa pine often develop.

Robert Fire of 2003

How to Use This Book

This book provides the reader with an overview of the 300 most common plant species in Glacier National Park, selected from 1132 different species that occur here. In making these selections the authors' intention was to keep the book light enough to toss into a daypack, yet infomative enough to make it worth the extra weight. Therefore, plants will be encountered along a hike that are not in this book. If a plant is common in a particular area but is not in the book, it may be locally common in that site but not widespread in the park. The "Selected References" section at the end of this book provides a list of field guides and other plant-related works that may also be helpful in species identification.

Plant species in this book have been grouped according to flower color. Flower color, however, is in the eye of the beholder. A flower that is pink to one person may be obviously purple to another. In addition to this complication, certain plants may produce light pink flowers in one site and white flowers in a different location. Flower color is also influenced by moisture availability in some species. Therefore, it is advisable to check several color sections when searching for the identity of a particular plant.

Guidelines and Safety Precautions

Wildflowers encountered along the trails and in the backcountry of Glacier National Park are best left for the enjoyment of all hikers. Picking flowers is not permitted in the park, nor is gathering a large quantity of berries. A handful of huckleberries here and there while hiking a mountain trail is perfectly acceptable, but harvesting for home use is best left for areas outside of the park.

References this book makes to edible and medicinal qualities of certain plants are meant to educate the reader. Experimentation with edible and medicinal plants is dangerous and should only be practiced under the guidance of an expert. **Collecting and using any part of a plant as food or medicine is not permitted in Glacier National Park and strongly discouraged by the authors.**

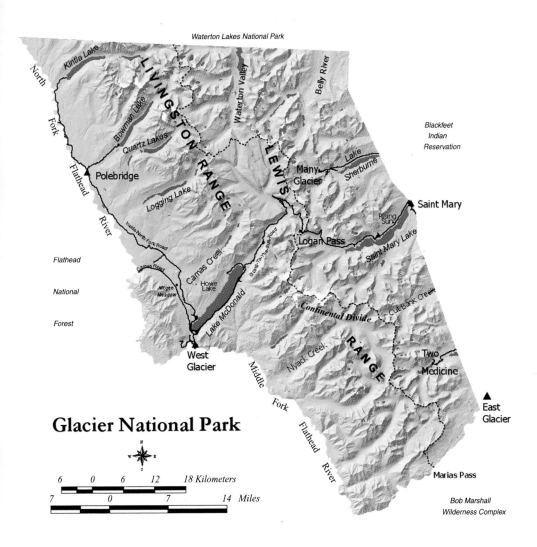

Waterton Lakes National Park

Blackfeet
Indian
Reservation

North

Fork

Flathead

River

Kintla Lake

LIVINGSTON RANGE

Bowman Lake

Quartz Lakes

Polebridge

Logging Lake

Inside North Fork Road

Camas Road

McGee
Meadow

Howe
Lake

Camas Creek

Lake McDonald

West
Glacier

Flathead

National

Forest

Waterton Valley

Belly River

LEWIS

Lake
Sherburne

Many
Glacier

Rising
Sun

Saint Mary

Saint Mary Lake

Logan Pass

Going-To-The-Sun-Road

Continental Divide

Cut Bank Creek

RANGE

Nyack Creek

Two
Medicine

East
Glacier

Marias Pass

Bob Marshall
Wilderness Complex

Middle

Fork

Flathead

River

Glacier National Park

6   0   6   12   18 Kilometers

7   0   7   14 Miles

WESTERN RED CEDAR
Thuja plicata
Cedar Family (Cupressaceae)

Description: Western red cedar is a coniferous tree with reddish brown, peeling bark and a broadly conical crown, growing up to 150 feet tall. The trunk is often buttressed at the base. Flat, spreading branches bear needles that are appressed, scale-like and overlap each other. The egg-shaped cones of western red cedar are 3–5 inches long and are borne on small branch tips.

Habitat: Moist to wet forests and along streams at lower elevations; a major component of the lush forests along Lake McDonald; occurs west of the Continental Divide.

Notes: The scale-like leaves of this tree make it one of the easiest to identify. Western red cedar usually occurs with western hemlock (pg. 22), another tree that prefers moist conditions. The wood of western red cedar resists decay, which made it a valuable resource for Native Americans. They used the bark and wood for many necessities, such as baskets, ropes and canoes. Old, fallen trees sometimes become "nurse logs" for western red cedar and western hemlock seedlings, providing a suitable environment for germination and growth. Western red cedar is also known as giant arborvitae, which comes from *l'arbre de vie*, "tree of life." Sixteenth century king Francis I of France gave the tree this name after a tea brewed from its foliage cured scurvy in the explorer Jacques Cartier and his crew.

SUBALPINE FIR
Abies lasiocarpa
Pine Family (Pinaceae)

Description: Subalpine fir is characterized by its spire-shaped crown and upwardly turned needles. This evergreen conifer generally grows up to 100 feet tall in mountain forests and is stunted, twisted and shrub-like at treeline. The pointed needles are 1–2 inches long and bear white lines of stomata on both the upper and lower surfaces. The seed cones have a distinct purple cast and disintegrate on the tree.

Habitat: Abundant in upper-elevation forests; dominant in most shrubby, timberline forests (krummholz).

Notes: Branches of subalpine fir that are held down by snow (near treeline) often take root and send up shoots which form new, shrubby trees. Snow mold sometimes forms on the crowns of smaller trees that are bound by snowpack until mid-summer, giving the branches a blackish, rotted appearance. The resin of this tree was used by the Blackfeet Indians to treat fevers and colds and as incense. Other tribes pounded the needles into a powder that was mixed with deer fat and used on a variety of open wounds. The needles of subalpine fir are high in Vitamin C. Grand fir (*A. grandis*) also occurs in Glacier National Park, but is much less common. The needles of grand fir are blunt and flat (not curved upward), and there are lines of stomata only on the lower needle surface.

DOUGLAS FIR
Pseudotsuga menziesii
Pine Family (Pinaceae)

Description: Douglas fir is a tall (up to 165 feet) evergreen tree with a pyramidal crown and spreading to drooping branches. The grayish bark on older trees has reddish brown furrows, while the bark of younger trees is smooth with small resin blisters. The needles are spirally arranged on branches, green to bluish green, and 1–2 inches long. Seed cones are narrowly oblong and bear 3-pronged bracts projecting from each cone scale.
Habitat: Montane forests and open woodlands; much more common west of the Continental Divide; look for Douglas fir along the north shore of Two Medicine Lake, in the North Fork Flathead River valley and lower McDonald Valley.
Notes: The foliage of Douglas fir is very fragrant, making it a popular choice for Christmas trees. Douglas fir cones fall to the ground intact, which is a handy feature for identifying this tree since the cones are so distinctive. If you think you may be looking at a Douglas fir but aren't sure, check the ground. If you find an intact cone with 3-pronged bracts (and the rest of the description fits) you can be sure it's a Douglas fir. The 3-pronged bracts are often likened to a mouse diving headfirst into the cone scale, exposing its hind legs and tail.

ENGELMANN SPRUCE
Picea engelmannii
Pine Family (Pinaceae)

Description: Engelmann spruce has a narrow, pyramidal crown and scaly, thin bark. Its foliage is bluish green in color, giving spruce-dominated forests a blue-green cast when seen from a distance. The stiff, sharply pointed needles are arranged in whorls on the branches. Seed cones are 1–3 inches long, reddish purple to light brown in color and hang downward from the upper branches.

Habitat: Subalpine forests and moist, montane bottomlands; occasionally forms shrubby, stunted krummholz forests at timberline.

Notes: Spruce foliage is prickly, while that of subalpine fir and Douglas fir is not. Engelmann spruce hybridize with white spruce (*P. glauca*), a tree typically found at lower elevation. Engelmann spruce are able to survive extremely cold temperatures, an adaptation that makes them well-suited to Glacier National Park's high country. The seeds of this tree are an important food source for many forest dwellers, including grouse, chipmunks and squirrels. The Cooley spruce adelgid, a small aphid-like insect, produces cone-like swellings (galls) on the branch tips of Engelmann spruce.

WESTERN LARCH
Larix occidentalis
Pine Family (Pinaceae)

Description: Western larch is a deciduous conifer with thick, furrowed bark. Mature trees may reach a height of 165 feet. The bright green, 3-sided, soft needles of this tree are arranged in bundles and emerge each spring.These needles turn bright yellow in the fall before they're shed. Seed cones are just over an inch long and reddish brown in color. They fall to the ground intact.

Habitat: Lower-elevation forests west of the Continental Divide; larger trees are often seen projecting above the forest canopy; does not tolerate shady conditions, so seedlings must germinate and grow in open areas.

Notes: Western larch seedlings are commonly found after a fire has eliminated the forest canopy. This sun-loving species grows fast so it can out-compete other tree species for sunlight. The thick bark that develops as the tree ages makes western larch less susceptible than many other tree species to wildfire.

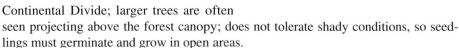

WHITEBARK PINE
Pinus albicaulis
Pine Family (Pinaceae)

Description: The branches of whitebark pine grow upward, forming a crown that is usually either round or flat-topped. Erect, tall trees (up to 70 feet) occur in sheltered forests, while twisted, shorter trees grow in more exposed sites. The bark is gray and scaly, and the yellowish green needles (1–3 inches long) are bundled into groups of 5. The egg-shaped seed cones (1½–3 inches long) are clustered at the tips of branches and are tightly closed until pried open by birds or small mammals. If left unharvested, the cones disintegrate on the tree branches.

Habitat: Subalpine forests and sparse, timberline woodlands; at treeline, often grows in shrubby, krummholz form.

Notes: Whitebark pine is in decline throughout most western states due to an epidemic of white pine blister rust. Stands of dead trees (inset) are common in the subalpine and treeline zones of Glacier National Park. Whitebark pine relys on one species of bird for seed dispersal: the Clark's nutcracker. These birds harvest seeds from whitebark pine cones and cache them in newly burned areas, where they often sprout as groups of seedlings. Trees that appear multi-stemmed are actually several trees that have sprouted from a nutcracker cache. Limber pine (*P. flexilis*) is a very similar and relatively uncommon five-needle pine that grows at lower elevations. The seed cones of limber pine are oblong and almost twice as long as those of whitebark pine. Limber pine cones fall to the ground intact, which is a good clue for differentiating between limber and whitebark.

LODGEPOLE PINE
Pinus contorta
Pine Family (Pinaceae)

Description: Lodgepole pine is a small (usually less than 65 feet tall), short-lived conifer with grayish brown, thin, scaly bark and a very straight, slender trunk. Its needles are
yellowish green, 2–3 inches long, and bundled into groups of 2. Egg-shaped seed cones,
1–2½ inches long, are green when young and golden brown at maturity. A large propor-
tion of these cones remain on the tree for many years. They are tightly closed and sealed
with a resin that melts at high temperatures (called serotinous cones).

Habitat: Low- to high-elevation forests; mixed with other tree species or in even-aged,
uniform stands; common in areas where fire frequency is relatively high, forming
"doghair" stands of closely spaced trees that are the same age and size; look for dense
lodgepole pine stands near Polebridge, a result of the 1988 Red Bench Fire.

Notes: Lodgepole pine relies heavily on fire for its reproductive success. The high
temperatures produced by fire open the seed cones of these trees, allowing thousands of
winged seeds to disperse. Lodgepole requires a lot of sunlight to grow and thrive, so a
freshly burned landscape makes the perfect home for a lodgepole pine seedling. As
these trees grow, the canopy of branches closes, reducing the amount of sunlight reaching the forest floor. This light reduction eliminates the chance that new lodgepole seedlings will survive, until the next stand-replacing fire occurs. As the stand ages, a self-
thinning process occurs when older trees die and fall. This creates openings in the canopy.
The resulting criss-cross of logs in the understory can be very difficult for hikers and
other animals to travel through!

WESTERN WHITE PINE
Pinus monticola
Pine Family (Pinaceae)

Description: Western white pine has a narrowly conical to slightly rounded crown that reaches a maximum height of 170 feet. The bark of mature trees is grayish and scaly. Soft, blue-green needles, 2–4 inches long, are bundled in groups of 5. Cylindrical seed cones are 6–10 inches long and mature after the second season. The cones are slightly curved and are attached to the branch by a small stalk. Cone scales are thin and tongue-shaped, bearing seeds with a conspicuous wing.

Habitat: Mixed lower-elevation forests west of the Continental Divide.

Notes: The long, curved cones of western white pine set this species apart from other conifers in Glacier National Park. The foliage is also softer than Glacier's other common pine species. The nutritious, oily seeds of this tree are an important food source for a wide variety of birds, including Clark's nutcrackers, grosbeaks, juncos and nuthatches.

PONDEROSA PINE
Pinus ponderosa
Pine Family (Pinaceae)

Description: Ponderosa pine has spreading branches and an open, conical crown up to 170 feet tall. The bark of mature trees is thick, furrowed and breaks into thin plates resembling jigsaw puzzle pieces. Needles are clustered on the ends of branches. They are 4½–8 inches long, yellow-green and bundled into groups of 3 (sometimes 2). Seed cones are broadly egg-shaped and 3–6 inches long. The cones are reddish purple when immature, gradually turning dull brown the second year after they are produced. At the end of 2 years, the cones fall from the tree. Cone scales are tipped with a stiff prickle.

Habitat: Drier habitats in valley bottoms; often found bordering grasslands, such as those along the North Fork Flathead River; also somewhat common in the lower McDonald drainage.

Notes: The thick bark of ponderosa pine protects these trees from periodic, low-intensity fire. Ponderosa pine is also a sun-loving species, requiring an open canopy to grow and reproduce. These trees thrive in areas that experience periodic ground fires that clear away brush and competing species that are less resistant to fire. The bark has a distinctive vanilla scent in the late spring and early summer. The scent is most apparent on days when the trunk has been warmed by the sun.

WESTERN HEMLOCK
Tsuga heterophylla
Pine Family (Pinaceae)

Description: Western hemlock has a nodding tip (inset) and downswept branches, giving this tree a feathery appearance. Its brown bark is thin and scaly. Shiny, yellowish green needles vary in size from ½–¾ inch long. They are flattened and arranged in two opposite rows. The narrowly oblong seed cones are ½–1 inch long and green when young. The cones turn brown as they mature, then fall to the ground intact.

Habitat: Moist to wet montane forests primarily around Lake McDonald; often grows with western red cedar.

Notes: Western hemlock thrives in shady, moist environments, and is not very resistant to fire. Native Americans used the soft branches of this tree for bedding and the strong wood for tools. Outside Glacier National Park this tree is harvested commercially and used in a wide variety of building applications, including cabinets, staircases, molding and doors. Beautiful ornamental cultivars of this tree decorate gardens throughout the northwest. Its common name is believed to come from European settlers who noticed that crushed foliage of western hemlock has a similar odor to poison hemlock (*Conium maculatum*), a member of the Parsley family. The specific name *heterophylla* is derived from *hetero*, or "variable," and *phyllum*, or "leaf," referring to the variable needle size.

PAPER BIRCH
Betula papyrifera
Birch Family (Betulaceae)

Description: Paper birch is a small, deciduous tree growing up to 50 feet tall. Its bark is gray when the tree is young. As it matures, its bark starts to peel and turns white, with dark horizontal lines adorning the trunk in a random pattern. Plants often have multiple trunks. The ovate leaves are 1½–3 inches long, toothed and narrowly pointed at the tip. Female catkins are 1–2 inches long when mature and bear tiny, hard, winged seeds.

Habitat: Moist, open, montane forests; readily sprouts in post-fire openings; common in the upper McDonald Valley on rocky slopes, especially in old burns; more abundant west of the Continental Divide.

Notes: The peeling bark from paper birch was used by many Native American tribes for items such as baskets and canoes. The wood was utilized for utensils and canoe paddles. Peeling the bark can scar or kill live trees and is illegal in Glacier National Park. The seeds are an important food source for birds, and ungulates browse the leaves and young shoots. Paper birch is a member of the fire-prone boreal forest that occurs across Canada. River birch (sometimes called water birch, *B. occidentalis*) is also a common tree in Glacier National Park, occurring along streams and swamps. River birch has gray to brown bark that peels little. Trees with peeling gray bark develop when river birch hybridizes with paper birch.

BLACK COTTONWOOD
Populus balsamifera
Willow Family (Salicaceae)

Description: Black cottonwood is a large, deciduous tree up to 130 feet tall with ascending branches and resinous, sweet-smelling buds. The bark is smooth and white to beige-colored on younger trees, becoming gray and deeply furrowed with maturity. The leaves are broadly lance-shaped and 2–6 inches long with toothed margins. They are shiny and dark green above and pale green beneath. Black cottonwood produces long, dangling clusters of tiny flowers (catkins). Male and female catkins are produced on separate trees, typically blooming in May. The female catkins of black cottonwood (pictured above) are 3–8 inches long, while male catkins are about 1 inch long.

Habitat: Moist to wet habitats from montane to subalpine; abundant along rivers, lakes and streams and in avalanche chutes on the east and west sides of the Continental Divide; common in moist aspen groves along the eastern edge of Glacier National Park.

Notes: Native Americans used black cottonwood leaves to heal skin lesions and muscle soreness, and the bark was chewed to ease cold symptoms. A tuft of hair on the seeds aids in dispersal. Streamside areas are often covered with tufts of the cottony seed in early summer. The resin-covered, new leaves fill the air with a spicy odor during early spring bud break. Moose, deer and elk eat the tender shoots and leaves in the spring.

QUAKING ASPEN
Populus tremuloides
Willow Family (Salicaceae)

Description: Quaking aspen is a deciduous tree growing up to 100 feet tall, often form-ing dense stands of similar-sized trees. Its bark is pale green to cream in color with scattered dark patches and lines. The leaf blades are broadly spade-shaped to round, 1–3½ inches long and pale beneath. Long, dangling clusters of tiny flowers (catkins) are formed in flower. Female catkins are 1½–4 inches long. Male catkins are smaller and are produced on separate trees. Fruit are oval capsules, about ¼ inch long, hanging in dense clusters.

Habitat: Abundant east of the Continental Divide, forming dense thickets of dwarfed trees in moist soil of shallow draws, drainages and depressions; less common west of the Continental Divide.

Notes: The leaves of quaking aspen "tremble" in the wind because the leaf petiole (stalk) is flat in cross section, versus round like that of most other trees. Its inner bark contains an aspirin-like compound (salicin) which has been used by herbalists to treat fever, inflammation and stomach ailments. Elk and deer browse the twigs and leaves of aspen. Elk feed on the inner bark, using their two lower front teeth to scrape off the bark and leaving vertical scars on the trunks. Fungal cankers are common in aspen. They cause decay of heartwood and provide nesting cavities for many birds, such as chicka-dees and woodpeckers.

BRACKEN FERN
Pteridium aquilinum
Bracken Family
(Dennstaedtiaceae)

Description: The fronds of bracken fern arise singly from spreading rhizomes. In spring the fronds first appear as "fiddleheads" before expanding and unfolding. Mature fronds are triangular in outline, 1–4½ feet long and pinnately divided two times into lobed leaflets that are narrowly lance-shaped in outline. The upper leaflet surface is hairless, but the underside is hairy. Some leaflets are fertile and bear a continuous line of spores along the outer margin. Leaf margins are slightly rolled under to protect the spores.

Habitat: Abundant in moist, montane forests and openings within forested landscapes; often colonizes disturbed sites, forming a dense colony.

Notes: Bracken fern was used as food by some Native American tribes, though many herbalists consider it to be poisonous. Fiddleheads are still used today as a potherb, but they must be boiled to remove the poisons. Some scientists believe bracken is allelopathic, preventing trees from recolonizing after a fire or clearcut.

LADY FERN
Athyrium filix-femina
Wood Fern Family (Dryopteridaceae)

Description: Lady fern leaf blades are 1–4½ feet long and tapered at both ends. They are pinnately divided 2 times into leaflets with deeply lobed margins. Several leaves may arise from a single point, giving the plant a vase-like appearance. The underside of fertile leaflets bear round or oblong spore clusters (sori) between the midrib and edge of the leaflet. A thin, crescent-shaped membrane (indusium) partly covers the sori, protecting spores from the elements until they mature and disperse.

Habitat: Common at all elevations in shady, moist sites such as avalanche chutes, wooded streambanks and moist to wet forests.

Notes: The crescent-shaped indusia distinguish lady fern from a similar species, male fern (*Dryopteris filix-mas*), which has indusia that are round in outline. The species name of lady fern, *felix-femina*, refers to its delicate, feminine fronds. Their outline is thought to resemble a woman's shapely leg.

FRAGILE FERN
Cystopteris fragilis
Wood Fern Family
(Dryopteridaceae)

Description: Fragile fern is a delicate, hairless perennial with tufts of leaves sprouting from spreading rhizomes. Each leaf is narrowly lance-shaped in outline and can grow up to 1 foot in length. Leaf blades are pinnately divided once into toothed leaflets. Each leaflet is deeply lobed. Circular spore clusters (sori) are produced on the underside of some leaflets, lying on top of veins that extend to the leaf edge. Sori are partly covered by a thin, hood-like membrane (indusium).
Habitat: Common on slopes with shallow, rocky soil and on rock outcrops at all elevations; requires shady to partially shady conditions.
Notes: The delicate indusium partially covering the spores of fragile fern is a protective membrane. This membrane shields the spores until they mature, then withers so spores can disperse. A similar species found in the same habitats is Woods fern (*Woodsia* species). Woods fern usually has more clustered leaves among conspicuous old leaf bases.

WESTERN OAK FERN
Gymnocarpium disjunctum
Wood Fern Family
(Dryopteridaceae)

Description: Western oak fern is a delicate perennial with leaves scattered along scaly rhizomes. Each leaf is approximately 16 inches long, triangular in outline and divided into 3 segments of similar size. Each triangular segment is pinnately divided 2 times into lobed leaflets. Fertile leaves bear circular spore clusters (sori) on their lower surface. Sori are positioned on veins near the leaflet edge.
Habitat: Common under moist, shady old-growth forest; often forms loose carpets among mosses; sometimes grows with lady fern (previous page).
Notes: The solitary, triangular leaves of western oak fern are very distinctive, setting this species apart from other common ferns in Glacier National Park. Look for western oak fern in the understory of mixed cedar and hemlock forests along the trail to Avalanche Lake.

HOLLY FERN
Polystichum lonchitis
Wood Fern Family
(Dryopteridaceae)

Description: Holly fern is an evergreen perennial, with strap-shaped leaves 2–20 inches long. Each leaf blade is pinnately divided into many lance-shaped, spiny leaflets. Fertile leaflets have 2 rows of circular spore clusters (sori) on their lower surface, located between the midrib and leaflet edge. Sori are covered with a protective, umbrella-like membrane (indusium) that arises from the sori center.

Habitat: Moist sites such as avalanche chutes, damp forests and wet, rocky slopes; common at all elevations.

Notes: Also called sword fern, this plant is common where running water keeps conditions wet much of the summer. Its generic name, *Polystichum,* comes from the Greek words *poly*, or "many" and *stichos,* or "row," describing the arrangement of sori on the lower leaf surface. Watch for holly ferns growing near waterfalls along Going-to-the-Sun Road. A similar species, common Christmas fern (*P. munitum*), is frequently seen along the Pacific slope of the Rockies but found only in the Lake McDonald area of the park. Its leaflets are at least 3 times as long as wide, while the leaflets of holly fern are less than 3 times as long as wide.

PARSLEY FERN
Cryptogramma acrostichoides
Maidenhair Fern Family
(Pteridaceae)

Description: Parsley fern is a small, delicate perennial with two distinctly different types of leaves: spreading to ascending sterile leaves and erect fertile leaves. The sterile leaves are 2–10 inches long and pinnately divided into egg-shaped leaflets. Fertile leaves are slightly longer and divided into linear leaflets. The edges of fertile leaflets are curled under, protecting a line of spore clusters on the leaflet underside.

Habitat: Sites with shallow soil, such as pockets of soil on rock outcrops or talus slopes; common at all elevations.

Notes: Parsley fern gets its common name from its resemblance to kitchen-variety parsley. It is also called rock brake.

MAIDENHAIR FERN
Adiantum aleuticum
Maidenhair Fern Family (Pteridaceae)

Description: Maidenhair fern has a fan-shaped leaf blade and a shiny, black petiole (leaf stalk). It often forms small colonies of plants where space and moisture are plentiful, sprouting from a horizontal or ascending rhizome. Arching to erect leaves are 4–24 inches long and wide. The leaves appear palmately divided, but are really pinnately divided 2 times into small leaflets. These leaflets have jagged margins and may be oblong or fan-shaped in outline. Crescent-shaped spore clusters (sori) are borne on the underside of fertile leaflets. Sori lie near the leaflet edge and are partially covered by the leaflet margin, which is rolled under.

Habitat: Common on wet cliffs or rock crevices from montane to subalpine, where moisture is present throughout the growing season; sometimes occupies damp forests.

Notes: Maidenhair fern is one of Glacier's most beautiful ferns. Its common name is reflected in its delicate, cascading appearance, which sets it apart from most other ferns in Glacier National Park. The generic name *Adiantum* comes from the Greek *adiantos* "repels water," referring to the fronds' ability to shed water.

GROUND-CEDAR
Diphasiastrum complanatum
Clubmoss Family (Lycopodiaceae)

Description: Ground-cedar is a low-growing, evergreen perennial with highly branched, flattened stems growing 4–10 inches tall. Its branches are cedar-like, with appressed, overlapping, scale-like leaves arranged in 4 rows. Cone-like structures (strobili), ¼–1¼ inches long, are produced at the tips of long (¼–3 inches) stalks. Strobili bear powdery spores within the axils of their fan-shaped, abruptly pointed bracts (or sporophylls).

Habitat: Common in moist forests from montane to lower subalpine.

Notes: Herbalists have used the spores of ground-cedar and other clubmosses to treat a variety of skin ailments, from diaper rash to eczema. Ground-cedar branches look very similar to branches of western red cedar scattered on the forest floor.

STIFF CLUBMOSS
Lycopodium annotinum
Clubmoss Family (Lycopodiaceae)

Description: Stiff clubmoss has creeping, evergreen stems that root at irregular intervals and a bottlebrush appearance. Solitary, upright shoots grow 2–10 inches tall and are usually unbranched. Needle-like leaves, up to ½ inch long, are dark green. Shallow teeth occur at the tip of each leaf. Cone-like structures ½–1½ inches long called strobili are produced at stem tips. Strobili bear spores in the axils of their egg-shaped, yellowish green bracts (or sporophylls). Each sporophyll has toothed margins and a hair-like projection at the tip.

Habitat: Common in shady, moist to wet forests from the valleys to lower subalpine; often forms loose carpets.

Notes: Stiff clubmoss is the most common species of clubmoss in Glacier National Park. Its spores have been widely used in the herbalist community to treat fever and inflammation and as antibacterial agents. Clubmoss spores are currently being studied for use in the treatment of Alzheimer's disease.

VIRGINIA GRAPEFERN
Botrychium virginianum
Adder's-tongue Family (Ophioglossaceae)

Description: Virginia grapefern is a delicate perennial herb with a single, erect stem growing 4–18 inches tall. Each plant produces a single, stalkless, sterile leaf (tropophore) that is broadly triangular in outline. It is pinnately divided 3–4 times into small, lobed segments and may grow up to 10 inches long. A modified, fertile leaf (sporophore) bears globe-shaped sporangia containing many tiny, yellow spores. The sporophore is pinnately divided 2 times, stands erect at the stem tip, and may be slightly shorter or longer than the tropophore.

Habitat: Common in dry to moist soil of coniferous forests and aspen groves in the montane zone; occurs on both sides of the Continental Divide, but is more common to the west.

Notes: The genus name *Botrychium* is derived in part from the Greek word *botrys*, meaning "a bunch of grapes." This description refers to the clusters of globose sporangia on the sporophore. Ten different species of grapefern grow in Glacier National Park. Most are uncommon and inconspicuous. Virginia grapefern is the most common and showy of these grapefern species.

COMMON HORSETAIL
Equisetum arvense
Horsetail Family (Equisetaceae)

Description: Common horsetail is a rhizomatous perennial with hollow stems. Stems have longitudinal ridges and are divided into sections connected at the nodes. A toothed, papery sheath circles the stem at each node. This plant has two growth forms: sterile (right side of photo) and fertile (left side of photo). Sterile plants grow up to 2 feet tall and have whorled branches, giving the plant a bottlebrush appearance. Fertile plants are tan-colored, unbranched and bear narrow cone-like structures, called strobili, at the tops of stems. Fertile stems are ephemeral, disappearing by midsummer. Spores are produced within the strobili inside umbrella-like structures called sporangiophores.

Habitat: Abundant at all elevations in moist locations such as streambanks, wet meadows, avalanche chutes and wet forests on the east and west sides of Glacier National Park.

Notes: A related species, scouring rush (*E. hyemale*), is also common in Glacier National Park. Scouring rush is a very robust plant, with thick, leathery, dark green stems up to 3 feet tall. Scouring rush has a single unbranched growth form. Silica in the stems of this species makes them abrasive, hence the common name. Horsetails (*Equisetum* species) are a food source for black bear and snow geese.

ROCKY MOUNTAIN MAPLE
Acer glabrum
Maple Family (Aceraceae)

Description: Rocky Mountain maple grows as a shrub or small tree up to 20 feet high. The gray bark is thin, and the new stems are reddish in color. The toothed leaves have a typical maple leaf shape, with 3–5 pointed lobes and a heart-shaped outline. Seeds are borne in pairs and have large wings that aid in their dispersal. In early fall the leaves turn bright magenta and eventually brilliant yellow toward the end of autumn.

Habitat: Montane to lower subalpine; especially common on rocky slopes, avalanche chutes, along streams and in moist forests where sun filters through the canopy.

Notes: Several horticultural varieties of Rocky Mountain maple have become ornamentals, adding color and visual interest to gardens throughout the northwest. Native Americans dried the wood of this tree for use in many tools, including bows, spoons and cradle frames.

SITKA ALDER
Alnus viridis
Birch Family (Betulaceae)

Description: Sitka alder is a deciduous shrub with arching, widespread branches up to 10 feet high. The alternate, oblong leaves are shiny green above, paler on the underside, up to 4 inches long and have sharp toothed margins. Winged seeds are borne in cone-like female catkins (roughly ½ inch long) which develop on new summer twigs. The winter buds are sharply pointed.

Habitat: Abundant in avalanche chutes and on steep slopes where its flexible stems bend rather than break; forms small patches in moist, open forest from montane to subalpine.

Notes: Mountain alder (*A. incana*) also grows in Glacier National Park. It has rounded winter buds, develops catkins on twigs of the previous season and is more common at low elevations. Native Americans used mountain alder for smoking meat and fish. Beavers use alder for food and lodge-building material.

MICHAUX'S MUGWORT
Artemisia michauxiana
Sunflower Family (Asteraceae)

Description: Michaux's mugwort is an herbaceous perennial with stems 7–27 inches tall. Its leaves are 1–2 inches long and pinnately divided 1–2 times into narrow segments. The foliage has a distinctive aroma when crushed. The upper leaf surface is smooth and green, and the lower surface is covered with a thick layer of white hair. Elongated, narrow clusters of flower heads are arranged along the top portion of the stem. Each flower head, less than ¼ inch high, is composed of a tight bundle of greenish flowers surrounded by green, leaf-like bracts. Michaux's mugwort blooms in July and August.

Habitat: Talus slopes, rock outcrops and exposed, stony slopes; common in subalpine and alpine zones.

Notes: Most members of this genus, *Artemisia*, are strongly aromatic when the foliage is crushed. Another, more familiar member of the *Artemisia* genus is big sagebrush (*A. tridentata*). Big sagebrush, a shrubby plant, grows on Glacier National Park's dry prairies along the North Fork of the Flathead River west of the Continental Divide. This genus was named for the Greek goddess Artemis, Apollo's twin sister.

BOG BIRCH
Betula glandulosa
Birch Family (Betulaceae)

Description: Bog birch is a deciduous shrub with erect, spreading branches growing 3–6 feet tall. Young twigs are covered with fine hair and bear distinctive wart-like resin blisters. The round to oblong leaves are ½–1 inch long, somewhat leathery and toothed along their margins. These leaves turn brilliant scarlet-brown in late fall. Erect female catkins (cone-like structures) are ½–1 inch when mature and bear tiny, hardened, winged seeds.

Habitat: Wet, organic soil of fens and marshes in the montane zone; occurs on both the east and west sides of Glacier National Park, but is more common west of the Continental Divide.

Notes: Despite its common name, bog birch does not grow in bogs in Glacier National Park. There are no true bogs within the Park (bogs receive moisture only through precipitation). There are, however, many fens (fens receive moisture from ground water), which provide excellent habitat for this species. This plant is also known as *B. nana*.

COMMON JUNIPER
Juniperus communis
Cedar Family (Cupressaceae)

Description: Common juniper is a mat-forming evergreen shrub growing up to 3¼ feet tall with short, sharp needles in whorls of three. The needles are whitish on the lower surface, dark green above and jointed where they meet the stem. Male and female cones occur on separate plants. The seed cones on female plants resemble berries and take two years to ripen. They are green the first year and turn purplish-brown the second year.

Habitat: Common in dry forest and exposed areas; often growing in Douglas fir or lodgepole pine woodlands and on rock outcrops; montane to subalpine.

Notes: Another juniper species that occurs in Glacier National Park is creeping juniper (*J. horizontalis*). Also an evergreen shrub, creeping juniper has prostrate stems and scale-like leaves that press against the stem. Rocky Mountain juniper (*J. scopulorum*, inset) is an erect shrub or small tree with ascending branches growing up to 20 feet tall. It has scale-like leaves pressed to the stem, similar to creeping juniper. All juniper "berries" are edible. Native Americans dried them and formed them into cakes for winter use. They were also used as a seasoning. Some people still collect and use the berries for meat seasoning and to give gin its distinctive flavor. Herbalists use juniper as a diuretic, cleansing the bladder and kidneys. A strong tea of the berries has been used to disinfect needles and bandages.

ALDER-LEAVED BUCKTHORN
Rhamnus alnifolia
Buckthorn Family (Rhamnaceae)

Description: Alder-leaved buckthorn is a deciduous shrub growing 1–6 feet high. Twigs are covered with short hair. The broadly lance-shaped leaves are 1–5 inches long with 5–7 prominent veins extending from the leaf base toward the tip. Leaves are arranged alternately along branches. Short-stalked, male and female flowers are produced on separate plants (dioeceous), arising in groups of 2–5 from the axils of lower leaves. They are green and less than ¼ inch wide with 5 sepals and no petals. Fruit are green at first, later turning black. They are berry-like drupes, each about ¼ inch long. This plant flowers in May and June.

Habitat: Abundant along marshes, swamps, lakes and fens; wet forest openings.

Notes: The berries of alder-leaved buckthorn are very poisonous. The bark contains compounds that have a laxative effect.

UNDERGREEN WILLOW
Salix commutata
Willow Family (Salicaceae)

Description: Undergreen willow is a deciduous shrub growing 8–60 inches tall with dark twigs covered with long hair. Its leaves are elliptic in outline, 1–3 inches long, sparsely long-hairy and the same color above and beneath. The leaf margins are shallowly toothed or toothless. Female catkins (flower clusters) are 1–2 inches long and produced on leafy stalks. Fruit are short-stalked, smooth capsules less than ¼ inch long with a tiny style projecting from the top. Mature catkins are produced in July and August.

Habitat: Abundant in moist soil along streams, ponds and wetlands near treeline.

Notes: Many willows have a waxy coating on the underside of their leaves called a "glaucous bloom." Undergreen willow doesn't have a glaucous bloom, so its leaves are the same color above and beneath. Booth's willow (*S. boothii*) also lacks the glaucous bloom. It is found at lower elevation and can be distinguished from undergreen willow by its smooth, hairless leaves. Another common willow, grey-leaved willow (*S. glauca*), is found in moist meadows and on limestone talus slopes in the subalpine zone. Grey-leaved willow does have the glaucous bloom previously mentioned, which is reflected in its specific and common names.

DRUMMOND'S WILLOW
Salix drummondiana
Willow Family (Salicaceae)

Description: Drummond's willow is a tall, deciduous shrub reaching 3–10 feet in height. Young twigs are usually grayish and waxy. Its leaves are green above and densely covered with silver hair on the underside. Leaf margins are toothless and slightly rolled downward. Leaves are narrowly elliptic to oblong in outline and 1–3 inches long. Flowers and fruiting capsules are clustered in erect catkins, 1–3 inches long. Capsules are hairy and about ¼ inch long. Drummond's willow produces mature catkins May to July.
Habitat: Moist, rocky slopes and river gravel-bars; bordering wetlands, streams, ponds and lakes; montane to just above treeline.
Notes: Drummond's willow is Glacier's most abundant willow species. The silvery, felt-like leaf underside is its most distinguishing feature. Many willows produce leaves with hairy lower surfaces when young, but this hair often falls off at maturity. It's critical to obtain mature leaves and catkins to accurately identify willows. A technical plant key is usually necessary. Drummond's willow is often one of the first plants to colonize freshly deposited gravels associated with retreating glaciers.

ROCK WILLOW
Salix vestita
Willow Family (Salicaceae)

Description: Rock willow is a low shrub with deciduous leaves and stems 8–40 inches tall. The leathery leaves are 1–2 inches long, elliptic to ovate in outline and have down-rolled margins. Leaves are deep green, distinctly veined above and covered with dense, white hair beneath. Flowers and fruiting capsules are clustered into erect catkins, 1–1½ inches long. Catkins are produced at the tips of twigs. Capsules are hairy and less than ¼ inch long, maturing in July and August.

Habitat: Abundant east of the Continental Divide on moist, rocky slopes and ridges and in wet meadows from subalpine to alpine.

Notes: Willows are notoriously difficult to identify. There are 23 willow species in Glacier National Park, many of which can only be separated by using a hand lens and technical plant key. Rock willow is an easy high-elevation willow to identify, distinguished by the impressed veins on its upper leaf surface and dense white hair beneath.

ARCTIC WILLOW
Salix arctica
Willow Family (Salicaceae)

Description: Arctic willow is a mat-forming shrub, rarely more than 3 inches tall, with deciduous leaves and trailing stems. Its leaves are ½–1½ inch long and narrowly elliptic in outline. They are shiny green above, waxy-pale on the underside and the leaf blade is tapered toward the petiole (leaf stalk). Flowers are grouped in erect clusters (catkins) of 25–50 on leafy shoots. Female catkins are typically ½–1¼ inches long. Female catkins mature into clusters of hairy capsules (each about ¼ inch long) in July and August.

Habitat: Abundant in moist soil of alpine meadows and turf and on exposed ridges and slopes; often found along streams or where snow lies late.

Notes: A similar species, snow willow (*S. reticulata*), is more confined to moist tundra. Snow willow has smaller catkins (less than ½ inch long), and its leaf blades are rounded at the base. Arctic and snow willow often grow together on moist sites at high elevations.

✕ DEVIL'S CLUB
Oplopanax horridus
Ginseng Family (Araliaceae)

Description: Devil's club is a deciduous shrub growing 3–7 feet tall with densely spiny stems. The large (4–12 inches wide) leaves have a distinct maple leaf shape and are densely spiny beneath. The greenish flowers (less than ¼ inch long) are produced on an erect, elongated stalk (raceme) 3–8 inches long. Berries, about ¼ inch long, are bright red and borne in showy, pyramidal clusters. Devil's club blooms in June and July.

Habitat: Most commonly found in moist to wet montane forests; may be encountered in avalanche chutes at higher elevation, primarily west of the Continental Divide; look for this plant near Avalanche Lake in the McDonald Valley.

Notes: The beautiful berries of devil's club are not edible and could cause a serious reaction if ingested. The inner stems were used by Native Americans to treat cold and flu symptoms. Root extracts were used by early Americans as a treatment for diabetes and have been proven to reduce blood sugar levels in laboratory animals.

BRONZE BELLS
Stenanthium occidentale
Lily Family (Liliaceae)

Description: Bronze bells is a slender perennial herb growing 4–20 inches tall from oval bulbs. Linear leaves 6–8 inches long arise from the plant base. Occasionally a smaller leaf or two grows at mid-stem. Nodding, bell-shaped flowers hang in loose clusters. Each flower is greenish brown, just over ¼ inch long and has 6 petal-like tepals. The tepals are fused into a tube toward the flower base and reflexed at the tip. The fruit is a capsule about ¾ inch long with 3 distinct beaks. Bronze bells blooms in July and August.

Habitat: Moist, shallow soil on shady cliffs and in mountain forests; montane to alpine.

Notes: Native Americans used this plant medicinally, but it is considered poisonous by modern-day herbalists and should not be ingested. The genus name *Stenanthium* comes from the Greek words *stenos,* or "narrow" and *anthos,* or "flower," referring to the plant's slender, delicate flowers. *Occidentale*, the specific name, means "from the west" or "from America," indicating the plant's origin.

GREEN FALSE HELLEBORE
Veratrum viride
Lily Family (Liliaceae)

Description: Green false hellebore is a robust, leafy perennial with hairy stems grow-ing 3–7 feet tall from thick rhizomes. Its pleated, twisted leaves are 4–12 inches long and elliptic in outline. They tightly clasp the stem. Yellowish green flowers are pro-duced in an open, branched arrangement. The branches, covered with flowers, spread and cascade downward. Each flower is composed of 6 petal-like, lance-shaped tepals, just over ¼ inch long. The fruit is a tiny, oval, three-chambered capsule. Green false hellebore blooms in July and August.

Habitat: Common in moist to wet, open forests, shrublands and avalanche chutes and in wet meadows where snow lies late; montane to subalpine.

Notes: Green false hellebore resembles corn stalks. These plants are extremely poison-ous and can be lethal in very small amounts. Even drinking water near green false hellebore plants can cause nausea, vomiting and constrained breathing. Native Ameri-cans experimented with this plant and uncovered powerful medicinal uses, particularly for convulsions, epilepsy, tonsillitis and pneumonia and as a heart sedative. It was a highly prized trade item between tribes. Early pioneers used a decoction of the leaves to rid themselves of head lice.

WESTERN TWAYBLADE
Listera caurina
Orchid Family (Orchidaceae)

Description: Western twayblade is a delicate perennial herb growing 3½–12 inches tall. A single pair of leaves are opposite one another at mid-stem. They are broadly elliptic and 1–3 inches long. Long-stalked, light green flowers are produced in a narrow array at the top of the stem. Each flower has 3 sepals and 2 petals that radiate in a star-shaped pattern. A lower, pear-shaped lip petal protrudes from beneath and is shallowly indented at the tip. Western twayblade typically blooms in July.

Habitat: Common in moist, shady forests from montane to lower subalpine; more common on the west side of Glacier National Park.

Notes: A related species, heart-leaved twayblade (*L. cordata*), grows in similar habitats, and the two are often found together. They resemble each other, but the lower lip petal of heart-leaved twayblade is narrow and deeply split into 2 slender lobes at the tip, and its leaves have shallow basal lobes that extend just around the stem. Sometimes these lobes make the leaves appear heart-shaped in outline; its specific name *cordata* refers to this character. Take the time to examine the tiny flowers up close; their delicate structure is truly beautiful. Twayblades are pollinated by mosquitoes.

MOUNTAIN SORREL
Oxyria digyna
Buckwheat Family (Polygonaceae)

Description: Mountain sorrel is an herbaceous perennial with a cluster of basal leaves and a leafless flowering stalk 2–16 inches tall. Kidney-shaped leaves are ½–2½ inches wide with long petioles. Inconspicuous, greenish red flowers are whorled around a slender, branched flowering stem. Seeds are contained within reddish, lens-shaped, winged fruits less than ¼ inch wide. Mountain sorrel blooms July to August.

Habitat: Abundant on rocky soil of outcrops, open slopes, moist meadows and ridges near or above treeline.

Notes: Mountain sorrel is rich in vitamins A, B and C and has a rhubarb-like taste due to the presence of oxalic acid. Native Americans added it to many different foods. Some tribes made a sauerkraut-like food by fermenting mountain sorrel in water. This preparation enabled them to store it for winter use. Herbalists have used it to treat digestive problems and skin ulcers, and its high vitamin C content makes this plant a good preventative for scurvy. Look for mountain sorrel in the rocky meadows around Logan Pass.

ALPINE MITREWORT
Mitella petandra
Saxifrage Family (Saxifragaceae)

Description: Alpine mitrewort is a delicate perennial herb with slender, leafless stems 6–14 inches tall. Its leaves are heart-shaped in outline, 1–2½ inches wide and palmately divided into 5–9 shallow, toothed lobes. Green, saucer-shaped flowers are loosely clustered in a spike-like arrangement. Each flower is composed of 5 reflexed to spreading sepals and 5 petals that are pinnately divided into 7–9 thread-like lobes. At the center are 5 stubby stamens, each lying at the base of a petal. This plant blooms June to August.

Habitat: Common in moist soil along streams, in wet meadows and forests and on sheltered cliffs from the montane zone to treeline.

Notes: A related species, common mitrewort (*M. nuda*, inset), grows in cool, swampy forests. Common mitrewort is easily identified by its 10 stamens positioned around the inside perimeter of each flower. Brewer's mitrewort (*M. breweri*) is common in the subalpine zone. Its 5 stamens are positioned at the base of the sepals versus at the base of the petals like alpine mitrewort. These plants were named for the Latin word *mitra,* or "cap," referring to the flower's cap-like structure.

STINGING NETTLE
Urtica dioica
Nettle Family (Urticaceae)

Description: Stinging nettle is a robust perennial herb with a square, grooved stem growing up to 4 feet tall. Lance-shaped, toothed leaves are arranged opposite each other along the stem. They are 3–6 inches long and armed with prickly, stinging hairs. Flowers are unisexual, greenish and tiny. They hang in loose, elongated clusters from the axils of upper leaves. Lacking true petals, the flowers have 4 tiny sepals, 4 stamens and 1 style. Stinging nettle blooms in June and July.

Habitat: Common in moist, rich soil at elevations up to subalpine; often colonizes disturbed soil, forming small colonies.

Notes: True to its name, stinging nettle produces an irritating rash if it comes into direct contact with skin. It produces various reactions. The irritation is not serious and usually clears up within a couple of days. As with most rashes, scratching can delay the healing process. Despite its reputation, stinging nettle has a vast array of medicinal and other uses. A tea made from it is used to treat respiratory, digestive and pulmonary disorders and is thought to alleviate anemia and skin problems. Cooking eliminates the stinging acid, making stinging nettle a good replacement for spinach.

X **ORANGE FALSE DANDELION**
Agoseris aurantiaca
Sunflower Family (Asteraceae)

Description: Orange false dandelion is a taprooted perennial with milky sap, growing 4–24 inches tall. The leaves are narrowly lance-shaped and smooth and may be shallowly lobed. The orange, solitary, dandelion-like flower heads perch at the top of leafless flowering stems. Fruit are one-seeded, slender achenes tipped with a long beak and a tuft of white bristles (pappus). Flowers typically appear in July and August.

Habitat: Open sites such as grasslands, meadows and rocky slopes at all elevations; grows on both sides of the Continental Divide, but is more common to the east.

Notes: Orange false dandelion is also commonly known as rafinesque and orange agoseris. Its thick, white sap contains rubbery latex compounds. Native Americans chewed the foliage of these plants like gum. Orange false dandelion has been used as an addition to salads like its cousin, the garden-variety dandelion. A yellow species of agoseris, yellow false dandelion (*A. glauca*, pg. 115), also grows in Glacier National Park in similar habitats.

PINEDROPS
Pterospora andromeda
Heath Family (Ericaceae)

Description: Pinedrops is a slender, reddish brown perennial herb with unbranched stems growing 8 inches to 4 feet tall. Its scale-like leaves primarily grow around the lower part of the stem. The leaves are purplish in color and about ½ inch long. Pendant, reddish orange to pale yellow flowers are well separated along the top of the stem, elongating as the inflorescence expands. Each flower is urn-shaped, about ¼ inch long and slightly sticky. Small, arching stalks connect the flowers to the stem. In fruit, a globe-shaped, brownish capsule is produced. Pinedrops typically blooms in August.

Habitat: Dry, often shady mountain forests, especially in the North Fork Flathead River valley.

Notes: Pinedrops are especially interesting plants because they lack chlorophyll, the compound that makes most plants appear green. Instead of producing the food they need through photosynthesis (using chlorophyll), pinedrops obtain food by digesting soil fungi that, in turn, obtain nutrition from their mycorrhizal association with coniferous trees.

PYGMY POPPY
Papaver pygmaeum
Poppy Family (Papaveraceae)

Description: Pygmy poppy is a small, tufted perennial herb with bristle-haired herbage and milky sap. The leaves are all basal, ½–¾ inch long and pinnately divided into rounded lobes. Solitary flowers are elevated on naked stalks well above the leaves. Each flower has 4 petals with a central ring of yellow stamens surrounding the ovary. In fruit this plant produces a bristly, conical capsule about ½ inch long. It blooms in July and August.

Habitat: Open, stony slopes and exposed ridges in the subalpine and alpine zones; occurs primarily east of the Continental Divide.

Notes: This plant is also known as alpine glacier poppy. Pygmy poppy is endemic to the Waterton-Glacier area, meaning it only occurs in our region of the northern Rockies. It is the only poppy species in Glacier National Park. The parabolic shape of its flower focuses the sun's rays toward the center, helping to speed fertilization and seed development once an insect has distributed pollen to the stigma.

ALPINE PAINTBRUSH
Castilleja rhexifolia
Figwort Family (Scrophulariaceae)

Description: Alpine paintbrush has a typical paintbrush appearance, with a red cluster of flowers at the stem top. It grows 4–16 inches tall. Lance-shaped leaves are 2–3 inches long, have entire margins (not toothed or lobed) and are arranged alternately along the stem. Leaf-like bracts subtend the flowers and are tipped with purplish red. The bracts often have 2–4 lobes at the tip. Flowers are purplish red, tube-shaped and 2-lipped, with a long, arching upper lip and a broad lower lip. Alpine paintbrush blooms in July and August.

Habitat: Abundant in moist soil of meadows in subalpine and alpine zones; less common at lower elevations.

Notes: Alpine paintbrush is very similar to common paintbrush (*C. miniata*), another abundant species in Glacier National Park. Common paintbrush typically has flower bracts with a distinctive scarlet color and usually grows at lower elevations than alpine paintbrush. Three red and four yellow species of paintbrush (*Castilleja* species) grow in Glacier National Park. Common paintbrush is usually scarlet but is occasionally whitish in color. See western yellow paintbrush (*Castilleja occidentalis*, pg. 151) for an example of one of Glacier's common yellow paintbrushes. All seven species are difficult to differentiate; a technical plant key may be required.

WHITE ANGELICA
Angelica arguta
Parsley Family (Apiaceae)

Description: White angelica often grows quite tall (stems can be 1–5 feet high) and has leaves that are twice pinnate (each leaf is divided into segments, which are further divided into smaller leaflets). Each leaflet is oval, 1–4 inches long and toothed along its margin. The flowers are white, very small and form a two-tiered, flat-topped inflorescence resembling an umbrella (compound umbel). White angelica blooms in July and August.

Habitat: Moist mountain forests and meadows; especially common in aspen groves and along streams.

Notes: The stems, roots and crushed fruit of white angelica have a distinct anise-like smell. This plant is an important food for both grizzlies and black bears throughout the summer.

COW PARSNIP
Heracleum sphondylium
Parsley Family (Apiaceae)

Description: Cow parsnip is a robust plant growing 3–7 feet tall with a hollow stem and large, palmate leaves up to a foot long. Leaves are divided into 3 segments, each 3-lobed like a maple leaf. The stem and leaves are covered with coarse hair. The flowers are white and arranged in umbrella-shaped flower clusters with flat tops (umbels). The fruits are heart-shaped, flattened and ¼–½ inch long. Cow parsnip blooms June to August.

Habitat: Moist, montane to subalpine, sheltered sites such as gentle avalanche chutes, streambanks and aspen groves.

Notes: Grizzly bears feed on cow parsnip in the spring when the stems are succulent. Native Americans used the inner stem and root of this plant as food. Herbalists prepare a tea from the dried root as treatment for nausea and indigestion. Look for this plant in the aspen groves along St. Mary Lake, just below Rising Sun.

MOUNTAIN SWEET CICELY
Osmorhiza chilensis
Parsley Family (Apiaceae)

Description: Mountain sweet cicely is an herbaceous perennial growing 1–3 feet tall from a thick taproot. Its foliage is sparsely bristly-hairy and sweetly aromatic when crushed. Leaves are triangular in outline and borne along the stem. Each leaf is divided 2 times into small, coarsely toothed leaflets, ½–3 inches long. Tiny, white flowers are arranged in loosely branched, open clusters at the stem tip. Black, club-shaped fruit are produced in the fall. Each fruit is ½–¾ inches long and hairy, with a short beak-like projection at the tip. Mountain sweet cicely blooms in June and July.

Habitat: Dry to moist mountain forests, avalanche chutes and streambanks; often grows in lush aspen groves.

Notes: The hairy fruits of mountain sweet cicely easily adhere to passersby, enabling this plant to readily disperse its seeds. All four species of sweet cicely (*Osmorhiza* species) found in Glacier National Park are aromatic. One can often smell this plant before seeing it, as its foliage, crushed underfoot, releases a sweet, anise-like scent. The generic name comes from the Latin *osmos,* "fragrant" and *rhiza,* "root," referring to the sweet smell of this plant's roots. Herbalists use a preparation made from the roots as a mild laxative.

BLACK SNAKE-ROOT
Sanicula marilandica
Parsley Family (Apiaceae)

Description: Black snake-root is a perennial herb with erect stems 1–3 feet tall. Its leaves arise from near the plant base. Each leaf is long-stalked and palmately divided into 5–7 coarsely toothed leaflets. Tiny, greenish-white flowers are arranged in a flat-topped group of hemispheric clusters. Each flower head is roughly ½ inch wide. Its fruits are oval, just under a ¼ inch long and covered with hooked prickles. Black snake-root blooms in June and July.

Habitat: Common in moist, rich soil of aspen groves, shrubby thickets and open forest.

Notes: Black snake-root has been used by Native Americans and herbalists for a wide variety of medicinal purposes. In keeping with its name, the plant was used when dressing snakebites. It was also used to treat skin ulcers, relieve sore throat and soothe anxiety.

DOGBANE
Apocynum androsaemifolium
Dogbane Family (Apocynaceae)

Description: Dogbane is a perennial herb with milky sap and stems 8–40 inches tall. The oval leaves are 1–4 inches long, pointed at the tip and borne opposite each other on the stem. The pink, bell-shaped flowers occur in open clusters at the top of the stem. Seed pods are bean-shaped, pendulous, and 2–6 inches long. Dogbane blooms in July and August.

Habitat: Rocky soil of open sites in the montane zone; usually occurs on rocky slopes where soil has been disturbed.

Notes: Toxins in the milky sap can produce skin irritation and may be fatal if ingested. Fibers from the inner stem of this plant were used by Native Americans as thread and were woven together for bow strings.

WILD SARSAPARILLA
Aralia nudicaulis
Ginseng Family (Araliaceae)

Description: Wild sarsaparilla is a rhizomatous perennial growing 4–16 inches tall. The single leaf arises from a long petiole at the base of this plant and is twice divided, first into 3 parts, then into 3–5 leaflets per part. Leaflets are broadly lance-shaped, 1–5 inches long and have toothed margins. The inconspicuous, greenish white flowers are approximately ½ inch across and clustered in globe-shaped arrangements on a stalk shorter than the leaf petiole. The dark purple berries are roughly ¼–½ inch in diameter. This plant flowers early in the spring, typically in May and June.

Habitat: Common in moist, sheltered montane forests on the west side of Glacier National Park; look for this plant along trails in the McDonald Valley.

Notes: The roots of wild sarsaparilla were used by Native Americans and pioneers as a beverage flavoring. Native Americans also used a poultice of wild sarsaparilla to treat fevers, stomachaches, coughs and skin ulcers. The berries have been known to produce illness when ingested. Its specific name, *nudicaulis,* means "naked-stemmed" or "leafless," referring to the leafless flowering stem.

✕ YARROW
Achillea millefolium
Sunflower Family (Asteraceae)

Description: Yarrow is a wooly, rhizomatous perennial that grows up to 2 feet tall. The slender, lance-shaped leaves are 1–6 inches long and divided 2–3 times, appearing fern-like or feathery. The foliage of yarrow is aromatic when crushed. Its tiny white flowers are tightly clustered into heads (characteristic of the Sunflower family) less than ¼ inch tall. The flower heads are arranged in an umbrella-shaped cluster at the stem tip. Yarrow blooms June to August.

Habitat: Meadows, grasslands, open forest, and rocky slopes at all elevations.

Notes: One of the most ubiquitous plants in Glacier, yarrow is adapted to survive in a wide variety of ecological niches. The medicinal values of this plant have been recognized and used for centuries. Tea made from the foliage has been used to treat colds, fevers and diarrhea. Compresses containing yarrow leaves have been used for earaches, burns and insect bites.

TRAIL PLANT
Adenocaulon bicolor
Sunflower Family (Asteraceae)

Description: Trail plant is a slender perennial growing 1–2½ feet tall. Its triangular leaves have wavy margins, are green and smooth above, and covered with white, wooly hair beneath. The tiny white flowers are less than ¼ inch long and clustered into small heads at the tips of long inflorescence branches. Seeds (achenes) are club-shaped and glandular, adhering to clothing of passersby. Trail plant blooms in June and July.

Habitat: Abundant in moist montane forests; much more common west of the Continental Divide than east.

Notes: The silvery undersides of trail plant leaves are exposed when hikers walk through patches of this plant, leaving a distinct trail and giving this plant its common name. This characteristic is reflected in its specific name *bicolor*, meaning "two colors" in Greek. Its generic name comes from the Greek *adena,* "gland" and *caulis,* "stemmed," referring to the sticky, glandular stems. Trail plant is more common along trails because hikers help disperse its seeds.

PEARLY EVERLASTING
Anaphalis margaritacea
Sunflower Family (Asteraceae)

Description: Pearly everlasting is a slender perennial with a leafy stem growing 7–27 inches tall from spreading rhizomes. Its foliage is white-wooly, especially on the leaf underside. The narrow, lance-shaped leaves alternate around the stem and are 1–4 inches long. They are predominantly basal, with only a few small stem leaves. Flowering heads appear "pearly" due to shiny, white, papery bracts that surround each flower cluster. The tiny, yellowish brown flowers are almost obscured by these papery bracts. Pearly everlasting blooms June to August.

Habitat: Moist to dry forests, shrublands and grasslands from montane to subalpine; often sprouts following disturbance such as fire or minor flooding.

Notes: Frequently used in floral arrangements, pearly everlasting maintains its pearly appearance well into the fall. Herbalists and Native Americans have used this plant to treat a wide variety of ailments. Modern herbalists use it to lower fevers, loosen chest congestion and as a sedative. Native Americans treated tuberculosis, headaches, asthma and skin abrasions with pearly everlasting. They also smoked the leaves as a tobacco substitute. This plant may be confused with pussy-toes (*Antennaria* species, see facing page and pg. 156), another genus within the Sunflower family.

WOODS PUSSY-TOES
Antennaria racemosa
Sunflower Family (Asteraceae)

Description: Woods pussy-toes is an herbaceous perennial growing 4–24 inches tall from spreading stolons (runners). The upper portion of its stem is dotted with small glands. Most leaves are arranged in a rosette at the base of each plant. A few smaller leaves grow in an alternate pattern along the stem. All are green and hairless above and white-wooly below. The basal leaves are egg-shaped and less than 2½ inches long. Stem leaves are lance-shaped and smaller. The whitish green flowers are clustered into heads, about ¼ inch high, with several per plant in an open arrangement. Woods pussy-toes blooms in June and July.

Habitat: Abundant in meadows and forests from montane to subalpine.

Notes: There are 14 different species of pussy-toes (*Antennaria* species) in Glacier National Park, and many are hard to distinguish from each other. Most species have clustered flower heads that look like a cat's paw, as reflected in the common name. The open inflorescence (flower arrangement) sets woods pussy-toes apart from other pussy-toes species. Woods pussy-toes also has the ability to grow under the shade of a forest canopy, a feature unique to this species of pussy-toes. This plant is also known as race-mose pussy-toes.

OXEYE DAISY
Chrysanthemum leucanthemum
Sunflower Family (Asteraceae)

Description: Oxeye daisy is a showy, rhizomatous perennial with a typical yellow and white daisy flower head. Spoon-shaped basal leaves are 1½–6 inches long and have toothed or lobed margins. The toothed stem leaves are smaller and grow in an alternate arrangement. The plant's flower heads are produced singly on stems up to 2½ feet tall. Flower heads are 1½–2½ inches in diameter with white ray flowers around the perimeter and a button of yellow disk flowers in the center of each head. Oxeye daisy typically blooms in July and August.

Habitat: This European weed is common along roads and in disturbed meadows on both sides of Glacier National Park.

Notes: Oxeye daisy prefers open, disturbed sites, so does not threaten the natural forest communities in Glacier National Park. Meadows, however, are at risk of invasion. Park staff closely monitor this weed to ensure Glacier's prairies and moist meadows remain weed-free. This plant is the wild progenitor of the garden "shasta" daisy. Its stem leaves are sometimes harvested outside Glacier National Park for use in gourmet salads. Herbalists use tea made from oxeye daisy leaves as a diuretic and astringent and to stop or prevent excessive bleeding.

ELK THISTLE
Cirsium hookerianum
Sunflower Family (Asteraceae)

Description: Elk thistle is a robust, short-lived perennial that grows to 3¼ feet tall and is covered with dense, long, white hair. Its deeply toothed leaves, which are up to 8 inches long and occur in a basal rosette and on the stem, gradually get smaller toward the top. Several flower heads are loosely arranged at the top of the stem. White flowers are densely clustered and mostly obscured by rows of leafy bracts that surround each flower head. These bracts are covered with dense, cobweb-like hair. Elk thistle blooms in July and August.

Habitat: Common on open, rocky slopes, meadows and in aspen groves at all elevations.

Notes: Elk thistle is one of two native thistles in Glacier National Park. The other species, wavy-leaved thistle (*C. undulatum*), has light purple flowers and leaves with wavy margins. Two exotic thistles that have found their way into the park are bull thistle (*C. vulgare*) and Canada thistle (*C. arvense*). These two purple-flowered species are common in disturbed, open areas. Past grazing in the Belly River area has resulted in the invasion of Canada thistle along the trail and in meadows near the ranger station. The wind-borne seeds of Canada thistle allow it to colonize moist, disturbed sites such as beaver dams far into the back country.

CUT-LEAVED DAISY
Erigeron compositus
Sunflower Family (Asteraceae)

Description: Up to 8 inches tall, cut-leaved daisy is a small, delicate, herbaceous perennial growing from a taproot. Its foliage is sparsely hairy and glandular. The leaves are mainly basal, up to 2½ inches long, and divided 2–3 times into very small, narrow segments. Stem leaves are smaller and not divided or toothed. The flower heads are typical of the sunflower family and are solitary on stem tips. The heads are ½–¾ inch in diameter, with white ray flowers lining the perimeter and a button of yellow disk flowers in the center. A row of green, leaf-like bracts surrounds the flower head. These bracts are hairy and glandular and often tinged with purple near the tip. Cut-leaved daisy blooms June to August.

Habitat: Open, rocky habitats, such as rock outcrops, talus slopes, old stream channels and grasslands with stony, sandy soil; common at all elevations.

Notes: There are sixteen different fleabanes (*Erigeron* species) in Glacier National Park, making it our largest genus within the Sunflower family. Cut-leaved daisy is easy to recognize because of its dissected, delicate leaf structure and small stature. Fleabanes can be difficult to separate from asters since both have white to purple ray flowers and yellow disk flowers. To differentiate between the two, examine the bracts surrounding each flower head (involucral bracts). The involucral bracts of fleabanes are arranged in 1 or 2 uniform rows, while those of asters are layered like roof shingles.

WHITE-FLOWERED HAWKWEED
Hieracium albiflorum
Sunflower Family (Asteraceae)

Description: White-flowered hawkweed is a slender perennial growing up to 2 feet tall with milky sap and foliage sparsely covered with long hair. Its oblong leaves are 1½–6 inches long and mainly basal, and they may be shallowly toothed. Stem leaves become smaller toward the top. Flower heads are arranged loosely at the tops of stems. Off-white flowers are tightly clustered into a dandelion-like flower head about ½ inch in diameter. Surrounding the flower head is a row of small, leaf-like, often glandular bracts. White-flowered hawkweed blooms June to August.

Habitat: Abundant in meadows, shrublands and forests in the subalpine zone and just below; often growing with huckleberry (pg. 164) and beargrass (pg. 82).

Notes: White-flowered hawkweed is Glacier's only hawkweed with white flowers. Other hawkweed species growing in the park have yellow or orange flowers and usually occur in sunnier habitats.

MINER'S CANDLE
Cryptantha celosioides
Borage Family (Boraginaceae)

Description: Miner's candle is a short-lived perennial (sometimes a biennial) with stiff hair covering the stem and leaves and a flowering stem up to 12 inches tall. Its basal leaves are 1–2½ inches long, spoon-shaped, and clustered into a rosette. Stem leaves are smaller and narrower. White to cream-colored flowers with yellow throats are produced in an elongated cluster toward the top of the flowering stem. Each flower is ¼–½ inch wide and has 5 slightly reflexed petals. In fruit this plant produces 4 hard nutlets tightly clustered in the very center of the flower. Each nutlet is less than ¼ inch long and has a bumpy texture. Miner's candle blooms in June and July.

Habitat: Sparsely vegetated, stony soil of mountain meadows and slopes; occurs east of the Continental Divide.

Notes: Two true perennial species within the genus *Cryptantha* closely resemble miner's candle: *C. sobolifera* and *C. spiculifera*. The 3 species, closely related, are all referred to as "miner's candle." *C. celosoides* usually has a single rosette, while *C. sobolifera* and *C. spiculifera* usually have several rosettes, only some of which bear flowering stems. *C. sobolifera* is typically found at higher elevations than *C. spiculifera*.

REFLEXED ROCKCRESS
Arabis holboellii
Mustard Family (Brassicaceae)

Description: Reflexed rockcress is an erect, slender perennial with stems growing up to 28 inches tall. Its foliage is covered with fine, branched hair. Basal leaves form a rosette. They are oblong in outline, up to 2 inches ·long and finely toothed along their margins. Stem leaves are narrowly lance-shaped and clasp the stem. They are smaller than the basal leaves and are arranged in an alternate pattern along the stem. Clusters of white flowers sometimes tinged with purple or pink are arranged along the top portion of the stem. Each flower has 4 spreading petals, each of which is less than ½ inch long. Flattened pods 1–3 inches long are produced when the plant sets fruit. They are linear in outline and may be reflexed at an angle or hang down from a short stalk. Reflexed rockcress blooms in May and June.

Habitat: Well-drained, sparsely vegetated soil of open sites in the montane zone; common in grasslands, woodlands and on rocky slopes and streambanks.

Notes: The leaves of rockcress are edible. They are most commonly used as an addition to salads. There are ten species of rockcress (*Arabis* species) in Glacier National Park. All have 4-petaled flowers (ranging in color from white to pinkish purple), and all but one grow in dry soil of grasslands and outcrops.

NUTTALL'S ROCKCRESS
Arabis nuttallii
Mustard Family (Brassicaceae)

Description: Nuttall's rockcress is a very small, perennial herb growing up to 8 inches high, with sparsely hairy herbage. Spoon-shaped leaves are arranged in a basal rosette and bear long hair along the margins. Stem leaves are smaller and lance-shaped. White, 4-petaled flowers roughly ¼ inch in diameter are loosely clustered at the top of each stem. Fruit are linear pods ½–¾ inch long on spreading to erect stalks. The plant blooms in May and June.

Habitat: Dry soil of grasslands, meadows and rock outcrops from montane to subalpine; look for this plant in sparsely vegetated soil along St. Mary Lake.

Notes: This tiny plant is easy to miss when looking for showy wildflowers. Nuttall's rockcress is the shortest rockcress (*Arabis*) species in Glacier National Park.

✕ PENNSYLVANIA BITTERCRESS
Cardamine pensylvanica
Mustard Family (Brassicaceae)

Description: Pennsylvania bittercress is an annual or biennial herb with a branching stem up to 20 inches tall. Its basal leaves are 1–3 inches long and pinnately divided into 2–8 pairs of oval leaflets. A larger, broad leaflet is produced at the leaf tip. Stem leaves grow in an alternate pattern and are pinnately divided into narrow leaflets. White, 4-petaled flowers are borne in a loose, elongated cluster at the top of the stem. Each flower is less than ¼ inch wide. Narrow, ascending pods are produced in fruit. Each pod is flattened, ½–1 inch long and very slender. Pennsylvania bittercress blooms in June and July.

Habitat: Common in moist sites with sparse vegetation, mainly west of the Continental Divide; along wetlands, ponds and streams in the montane zone.

Notes: Bittercresses (*Cardamine* species), including this species, are sometimes used to infuse a peppery flavor in salads, soups and other dishes. Native Americans and early settlers used these plants to relieve or cure a wide variety of illnesses. They were thought to cure epilepsy, scurvy, asthma and urinary tract problems and to relieve cold and flu symptoms. Many species of mustard, including bittercresses, contain compounds that are thought to prevent the growth of cancerous cells.

ALPINE SMELOWSKIA
Smelowskia calycina
Mustard Family (Brassicaceae)

Description: Alpine smelowskia is a tufted perennial herb growing from a branched rootcrown, sometimes creating mats of small plants with stems up to 8 inches. The foliage is covered with dense, branching hair, giving the plant a grayish cast. Leaves primarily grow from the plant base and are up to 2 inches long. They are pinnately divided into narrow segments. Flowers are congested at the top of flowering stems. The flower is composed of 4 white petals, each roughly ¼ inch long. When the plant sets fruit it produces oval pods less than ½ inch long on erect stalks. Alpine smelowskia blooms in June and July.

Habitat: High elevation ridges, rock outcrops, talus slopes and moraines.

Notes: Soon after the snow melts in the alpine zone, tundra plants of that habitat must bloom to take advantage of the short summer season. Alpine smelowskia contributes to the showy display of these high-elevation cushion plants in midsummer. Look for it in suitable habitats along the Highline Trail.

UTAH HONEYSUCKLE
Lonicera utahensis
Honeysuckle Family (Caprifoliaceae)

Description: Utah honeysuckle is a deciduous shrub with branched, leafy stems 3–6 feet tall. Its oblong leaves are 1–3 inches long, entire (not toothed) and have a blunt tip. They are arranged opposite each other along the twigs. The cream-colored flowers are paired, growing from the joint between leaf and stem, and are often hidden underneath the leaves. Flowers are broadly tube-shaped with a bulge at the base. Pairs of bright red berries are produced in late summer. They are each about ¼ inch wide and are fused at the base. Utah honeysuckle blooms in June and July.

Habitat: Moist sites with intermittent sun, such as open forest, streambanks and sheltered shrublands; common both east and west of the Continental Divide.

Notes: The flowers of plants in the honeysuckle family have a characteristic tube-shaped flower composed of fused petals. Utah honeysuckle berries are edible, with a juicy texture and pleasant flavor.

BLACK ELDERBERRY
Sambucus racemosa
Honeysuckle Family (Caprifoliaceae)

Description: Black elderberry is a deciduous shrub growing up to 10 feet tall, with a distinctly unpleasant smell. Its branches often have a waxy coating. The leaves grow opposite each other along the branches. Each leaf is pinnately divided into 5–9 lance-shaped, toothed leaflets. Leaflets range in length from 2–6 inches and come to a slender, tapered point. Tiny, cream-colored flowers are arranged in a pyramid-shaped cluster at the tips of branches. Each flower is saucer-shaped and less than ¼ inch wide. The plant produces shiny, black berries just under ¼ inch wide. Black elderberry blooms in June and July.

Habitat: Common in shrubby thickets, avalanche chutes and moist, open forest.

Notes: Black elderberry fruit has been used in wine and jam for centuries. The uncooked fruits, however, have been reported to cause nausea and are considered poisonous by some sources. The roots, bark, leaves and stem have compounds with verified toxicity.

THREAD-LEAVED SANDWORT
Arenaria capillaris
Pink Family (Caryophyllaceae)

Description: Thread-leaved sandwort is a tufted perennial with linear leaves and flowering stems up to 8 inches high. The stem is glandular and finely hairy near the flowering portion of the plant. The stem leaves are soft and needle-like, 1–1½ inches long, and grow opposite each other along the stem. Basal leaves are longer, growing in tufts that sometimes create loose mats. The white, 5-petaled flowers are ¼–½ inch in diameter and grow in flat-topped clusters at the top of stems. Seeds are borne within egg-shaped capsules. Thread-leaved sandwort blooms in July and August.

Habitat: Stony soil of exposed ridges, rocky slopes and sparsely vegetated grasslands; abundant in alpine and subalpine zones; less common at lower elevations.

Notes: The basal leaves of thread-leaved sandwort sometimes look like tufts of short bunchgrass growing in rocky soil. Another alpine sandwort, ballhead sandwort (*A. congesta*), is very similar to thread-leaved sandwort, but its inflorescence is not glandular and its white flowers are crowded into a ball-shaped cluster. Ballhead sandwort is less common than thread-leaved sandwort in Glacier National Park. The generic name *Arenaria* comes from the Latin word *arena*, meaning "sand." The name refers to the preference many of these species have for sandy soil.

FIELD CHICKWEED
Cerastium arvense
Pink Family (Caryophyllaceae)

Description: Field chickweed is a perennial with hairy, often glandular herbage growing up to 12 inches tall. Mats of plants often form along trailing stems. Lance-shaped leaves grow opposite each other on the stem and are ½–1¼ inches long. Smaller leaves protrude from lower leaf axils. The white flowers, ¼–½ inch in diameter, are composed of five 2-lobed petals. The fruit is a capsule that is often curved at maturity. In the fall the capsule opens by forming 10 slits, through which the seeds are dispersed. Field chickweed blooms in June and July.

Habitat: Dry soil of open woodlands, grasslands, ridges and slopes in the montane zone; gravelly soil of alpine and subalpine meadows.

Notes: The small leaves growing from leaf axils set this plant apart from a similar species, alpine chickweed (*C. beeringianum*). Alpine chickweed grows only at high elevations in turf and rocky, sparsely vegetated habitats. The common name chickweed comes from the early European practice of feeding this plant to chickens and other domestic fowl. The generic name *Cerastium* is derived from the Greek word *keras*, meaning "horn," referring to the shape of the seed capsules.

ALPINE SANDWORT
Minuartia obtusiloba
Pink Family (Caryophyllaceae)

Description: Alpine sandwort is a low-growing, herbaceous perennial with stems up to 4 inches tall and glandular-hairy herbage. Its linear, needle-like leaves are about ¼ inch long and grow in tufts from a branched rootcrown. White flowers are produced singly at the tops of stems and are about ½ inch in diameter. Seeds are contained within capsules less than ¼ inch long that appear in the fall. Three slits form in the capsule to release seeds. Alpine sandwort blooms in July and August.

Habitat: Sparse, stony soil of alpine and subalpine meadows, rocky slopes and exposed ridges; primarily found above treeline.

Notes: The plants in this genus (*Minuartia*) were once included in the genus *Arenaria*. They share the common name sandwort, referring to the sandy habitat that many of the species prefer. The tufted growth form of these tiny alpine plants reduces heat and water loss, enabling them to survive and often thrive in harsh conditions. Rocky Mountain sandwort (*M. rossii*) and Nuttall's sandwort (*M. nuttallii*) resemble alpine sandwort and grow in similar habitats. Rocky Mountain sandwort is distinguished by its tufted growth form, sharply pointed sepals and smooth, hairless foliage. Nuttall's sandwort also has pointed sepals, but it grows in mats and has glandular-hairy foliage. This genus (*Minuartia*) is named after Spanish botanist Juan Minuart (1693–1768). The specific name of alpine sandwort, *obtusaloba*, comes from the Latin *obtusus* meaning "blunted or dulled," referring to the shape of the sepal tips.

PARRY'S CAMPION
Silene parryii
Pink Family (Caryophyllaceae)

Description: Parry's campion is an erect, slender perennial with stems growing 8–20 inches tall from a branched rootcrown. The plant's herbage is covered with short hair and the upper portion of the stem is sticky. Its leaves are narrowly oval and 1-3 inches long. They are produced at the base of the plant and opposite each other along the stem. White flowers, sometimes tinged with purple, grow in a loose cluster at the top of the plant. Each showy, tubular flower is about ¾ inch wide, with 5 petals that are deeply 4-lobed. The calyx is striped. Parry's campion blooms in July and August.

Habitat: Open sites such as grasslands, meadows and woodlands; occurs on both sides of the Continental Divide at all elevations, but is more common to the west.

Notes: The frilly petals of Parry's campion are very distinctive. Some members of this genus (*Silene*) are called "catchfly" because small insects stick to the glandular, sticky portions of the stem and flowers.

LONG-STALKED CHICKWEED
Stellaria longipes
Pink Family (Caryophyllaceae)

Description: Long-stalked chickweed is a rhizomatous perennial with smooth, hairless foliage and a slight blue tinge. Its stems grow 2–12 inches tall, sometimes forming small mats of plants. Narrowly lance-shaped leaves are ½–1¼ inches long, pointed at the tip, and produced opposite each other along the stem. One to several white flowers are produced at the top of each flowering stem. The flowers are about ½ inch wide and are composed of 5 deeply lobed petals. Sometimes the petals are notched so close to the base that the flower appears to have 10 narrow petals. This plant typically blooms in July.

Habitat: Moist soil of high-elevation meadows and slopes and near streams.

Notes: All chickweeds (*Stellaria* species) are considered edible and are used most often as salad greens. Herbalists have prescribed chickweed for digestive ailments and skin irritation. A related species, northern chickweed (also called northern starwort, *S. calycantha*), resembles long-stalked chickweed and grows in similar habitats. Northern chickweed lacks the bluish tinge of long-stalked chickweed, and its flowers are much smaller.

BUNCHBERRY
Cornus canadensis
Dogwood Family (Cornaceae)

Description: Bunchberry is a low-growing, rhizomatous perennial 2–8 inches tall with a woody base. Its evergreen, oval leaves are 1–2½ inches long and have prominent veins running almost parallel to each other. Several leaves are whorled around the stem at a single point. Four large, white, petal-like bracts subtend the flower cluster at the tip of each stem. Tiny, white flowers are tightly clustered in the middle of these oval bracts. Bright red berries 2½–3 inches long are produced in the fall and form a cluster at the top of the plant. Bunchberry blooms in June and July.

Habitat: Common in the understory of moist, shady forests and shrublands from montane to subalpine.

Notes: The four showy, white bracts that surround bunchberry flowers are often mistaken for its flower petals. They are actually modified leaves used to attract passing pollinators to the central cluster of inconspicuous white flowers. The bright red berries create a beautiful display in the fall and are an important food source for birds and small mammals. Humans can also eat bunchberries, but they aren't very flavorful, and unripe berries have been reported to cause stomachaches. Native Americans had several medicinal uses for this plant. A tea made from the roots was given to colicky infants; boiled and strained berries were used to treat paralysis; and a poultice of crushed berries was applied to treat minor burns.

RED OSIER DOGWOOD
Cornus sericea
Dogwood Family (Cornaceae)

Description: Red osier dogwood is a tall shrub (3–10 feet high) with deciduous leaves and thin, dark red bark. Its leaves are oval, 1-6 inches long and hairy on the underside. Long, prominent veins run the length of the leaf parallel to the leaf margin. Flowers are arranged in an open, flat-topped cluster at the ends of branches. Each white, 4-petaled flower is less than ¼ inch in diameter. In the fall this plant produces white, berry-like fruit. Each fruit is about ¼ inch wide and contains a single seed. Red osier dogwood blooms May to July.

Habitat: Abundant in moist, partially open sites such as streambanks and avalanche chutes; common in moist to wet forests; occurs primarily in the montane zone.

Notes: Glacier's plants are *Cornus sericea* subspecies *stolonifera*, and some botanists call the plant *Cornus stolonifera*. The Blackfeet Tribe collected and smoked the inner bark of red osier dogwood alone or mixed with tobacco. The Blackfeet also used the inner bark to treat liver problems, and the berries were used for food. Other tribes outside Glacier National Park used the roots to treat diarrhea and as an astringent. Tribes across North America used the strong wood of red osier dogwood for arrows, digging sticks and other tools. Moose browse this shrub heavily, and a wide variety of animals eat the berries, including birds and black bears. Humans can eat the berries, but they have a foul flavor, so are best considered an emergency food.

ROUND-LEAVED SUNDEW
Drosera rotundifolia
Sundew Family (Droseraceae)

Description: Round-leaved sundew is a small, delicate, insect-eating perennial with stems up to 7 inches tall. Its round leaves form a rosette at the plant base. The leaf blades are ¼–½ inch long, and leaf stalks are ½–2½ inches long. Reddish purple, gland-tipped hairs cover the upper leaf surface and fringe the margin. White, inconspicuous flowers are produced in a loose, one-sided cluster at the top of the flowering stem. Each flower has 5 tiny petals and an overall diameter less than ¼ inch. Round-leaved sundew blooms in July and August.

Habitat: Limited to wet soil of *Sphagnum* fens in the montane zone; common west of the Continental Divide and in the Waterton Valley.

Notes: The gland-tipped hairs that line the upper leaf surface of round-leaved sundew enable this plant to capture and digest small insects. Insects that land on these leaves are trapped in a sticky substance produced by the glands. The insect's struggle triggers the plant to curl its leaves, pressing more glands against the insect's body. Digestive enzymes secreted by the glands dissolve the insect body into an absorbable liquid that is taken up by the leaf. The exoskeletons of devoured insects are often observed on the leaves of this plant.

LABRADOR TEA
Ledum glandulosum
Heath Family (Ericaceae)

Description: Labrador tea is an evergreen shrub with erect branches growing 1–2 feet tall. Its hairy twigs are reddish in color and often dotted with tiny glands. Oval to elliptic leaves grow in an alternate pattern along the stem. Leaves are leathery, ½–3 inches long and slightly rolled under along the margin. The upper leaf surface is shiny and the lower surface is speckled with small resin glands. White, dish-shaped flowers are clustered at the tips of branches. Each flower is about ½ inch wide, 5-petaled and has 8–12 long, thread-like stamens. This plant blooms in May and June.

Habitat: Common in moist soil of mountain swamps, shrub thickets and spruce forest; often forms a ring around wetlands just upland from saturated soil; occurs west of the Continental Divide.

Notes: Native peoples and early Americans boiled the leaves of this plant into tea. Too much Labrador tea, however, is considered toxic, causing digestive discomfort and drowsiness. Herbalists use the plant to treat cold symptoms, nervousness, and lice.

ONE-SIDED WINTERGREEN
Orthilia secunda
Heath Family (Ericaceae)

Description: One-sided wintergeen, a perennial herb, grows from spreading rhizomes (underground stems), with flowering stems up to 8 inches high. The shiny, evergreen leaves grow low on the stem, appearing basal. They are egg-shaped or sometimes round in outline, finely toothed and ½–2 inches long. A single stem bears a row of nodding, bell-shaped flowers all hanging from one side. The flowers are whitish green and less than ¼ inch in diameter. One-sided wintergreen blooms in July and August.

Habitat: Shady, relatively moist forests from montane to subalpine; occurs on both the east and west sides of the Continental Divide.

Notes: This plant is also known as *Pyrola secunda*. The Blackfeet Indians used an infusion of the roots and leaves of one-sided wintergreen as a mild laxative and a treatment for chest colds in children. Herbalists use the leaves for such skin ailments as rashes, blisters and insect bites.

AMERICAN MILK-VETCH
Astragalus americanus
Pea Family (Fabaceae)

Description: American milk-vetch is a robust perennial with erect stems 20 inches to 3 feet tall. Its foliage is smooth and hairless. Leaves are arranged in an alternate pattern along the stem and are pinnately divided into 7–17 elliptic leaflets. Each leaflet is ½–2 inches long and ¼–½ inch wide. Many yellowish white flowers are clustered at the top of the flowering stem in an elongated arrangement (raceme). Each flower is about ½ inch long and composed of a large, upper banner petal, 2 lateral wing petals and 2 lower keel petals that are united along the bottom. The flowers droop down from the point of stem attachment. When this plant sets fruit it produces slender, hanging pods, ½–1 inch long and about ¼ inch wide. American milk-vetch typically blooms in July.

Habitat: Open forests and shrublands in the montane zone; often in aspen groves.

Notes: Some milk-vetch (*Astragalus*) species are poisonous due to their ability to absorb and concentrate naturally occurring soil compounds such as selenium. Livestock grazing in areas where milk-vetches are common have been fatally poisoned. The degree of plant toxicity depends to a large degree on the amount of toxic compound in the soil. American milk-vetch is not considered poisonous, but all vetch species should be avoided since they are hard to differentiate.

WHITE GERANIUM
Geranium richardsonii
Geranium Family (Geraniaceae)

Description: White geranium is a robust perennial growing 15–35 inches tall. The lobed leaves are round in outline and 2½–6 inches wide. The sepals (green, outer flower parts) are glandular and sticky. The flower petals, ½–¾ inch long, are white with purple veins and form a 5-lobed, saucer-shaped flower. Long, linear capsules bear seeds and are produced in late summer and fall. White geranium blooms in July and August.

Habitat: Partial shade of moist, montane forests and shrub thickets; especially common under aspen; primarily found east of the Continental Divide but occasionally seen in the Middle Fork Flathead drainage.

Notes: The genus name *Geranium* is derived from the Greek word for "crane," *geranos*, referring to the long, beak-like fruit of these plants.

STICKY CURRANT
Ribes viscossisimum
Gooseberry Family (Grossulariaceae)

Description: Sticky currant is an erect shrub with branches growing 20–40 inches high. Branches lack barbs and bristles. Leaves are 1–4 inches wide, divided into 3–5 palmate lobes and covered with soft, glandular hair. Each lobe is shallowly toothed. Clusters of 3–7 bell-shaped, white flowers are produced along branches. Each flower is ½–¾ inch long and sometimes tinged with pink. Black berries, just under ½ inch long and sparsely covered with glands and hair, are produced in late summer. Sticky currant blooms May to July.

Habitat: Moist to dry forests, shrublands and avalanche chutes from montane to subalpine.

Notes: Another common currant in Glacier National Park is stinking currant (*R. hudsonianum*), distinguished from sticky currant by its sparsely hairy, aromatic leaves and glandular (but not hairy) berries. Stinking currant grows in moist mountain forests and along streams. The berries of sticky currant have been reported to cause nausea and vomiting even in small quantities. The Blackfeet Indians used an extract of currant roots to treat kidney problems.

MOCK ORANGE
Philadelphus lewisii
Hydrangea Family (Hydrangeaceae)

Description: Mock orange is a deciduous shrub with erect, loosely spreading branches and sweetly fragrant flowers. The broadly lance-shaped leaves are 1–2½ inches long and occur opposite each other along branches. They have mostly entire (toothless) margins and 3 prominent veins running from the base toward the tip. The aromatic flowers are white with yellow centers. Each flower has 4 petals and is about 1¼ inches in diameter. Seeds are borne in an elliptic, 4-chambered capsule ¼–½ inch long. Mock orange typically blooms in July.

Habitat: Dry, rocky slopes in the montane zone; common in the Middle Fork of the Flathead River valley west of the Continental Divide; occurs east of the Divide near St. Mary Lake.

Notes: This plant is also known as syringa. Mock orange has been cultivated as an ornamental shrub and easily grows in northern climates. It is the state flower of Idaho. Native Americans used mock orange medicinally to treat skin inflammation and ulcers, and to relieve chest pain. The stiff wood was used to make tools, basket frames and cradles.

MARIPOSA LILY
Calochortus apiculatus
Lily Family (Liliaceae)

Description: Mariposa lily, a delicate perennial herb with an unbranched stem 4–12 inches tall, grows from egg-shaped bulbs. A single, grass-like leaf arises from the plant base. The leaf is flat, ¼–¾ inch wide and typically shorter than the flowering stem. Bowl-shaped flowers are borne at the stem tip. Each is composed of 3 yellowish white, wedge-shaped petals and 3 narrow, green sepals. The petals are hairy on the inner surface, fringed along the edges and abruptly pointed at the tip. They often have a tiny purple spot near the base. In fruit, this plant forms a nodding capsule about 1 inch long. Mariposa lily blooms June to August.

Habitat: Common in dry soil of meadows, grasslands and open forest from montane to lower subalpine.

Notes: This plant is also known as pointed mariposa. Both Native Americans and early settlers used the bulbs of mariposa lily for food. They are known to be quite nutritious, with a sweet, potato-like taste. The generic name *Calochortus* comes from the Greek *kalos,* "beautiful" and *chortos,* "grass." The specific name *apiculatus* means "small-pointed," probably referring to the pointed anthers, petals and sepals. Look for this plant in the broad meadows near Rising Sun.

BEAD LILY
Clintonia uniflora
Lily Family (Liliaceae)

Description: Bead lily is a low-growing perennial spreading from extensive rhizomes, with leafless stems ¼–½ inch tall. It is sparsely covered with long hair, especially on the lower leaf surface and stem. The leaves are narrowly elliptic, 3–6 inches long and fleshy, arising from the plant base in groups of 2–4. A single, white flower is borne on the tip of each flowering stem. It has 6 petal-like tepals, each ½–¾ inch long. In fruit, a single, lustrous, blue berry is produced, about ½ inch in diameter. Bead lily blooms in June and July.

Habitat: Common in moist mountain forests throughout Glacier National Park, especially west of the Continental Divide.

Notes: This plant is also known as queen's cup. The solitary, glossy blue berry makes bead lily easy to identify in fruit. The berries look tempting but have a foul flavor and are considered inedible. Bead lily's leaves resemble those of glacier lily (pg. 140), but glacier lily leaves are hairless. The specific name *uniflora* means "one flower" in Latin, referring to the single flower produced by each plant. Look for bead lily in the moist, shady forests of the McDonald Valley.

ROUGH-FRUITED FAIRY-BELL
Prosartes trachycarpa
Lily Family (Liliaceae)

Description: Rough-fruited fairy-bell is a robust perennial with leafy, branching stems 12–32 inches tall from spreading rhizomes. The leaves are oval and 1½–5 inches long with pointed tips. They are hairy on the underside and along the margins but smooth and hairless on the upper surface. Narrowly bell-shaped, cream-colored flowers are produced at branch tips. The flowers are stalked, sometimes arising singly or in a cluster of 2–3. Each flower is about ½ inch long and composed of 6 narrow, petal-like tepals. The flowers hang downward and are sometimes obscured by leaves. The fruit are bright red to orange-yellow berries just over ¼ inch long with rounded tips and bumpy skin. Rough-fruited fairy-bell blooms in May and June.

Habitat: Abundant in moist mountain shrublands and forests.

Notes: A related species, Hooker's fairy-bell (*P. hookeri*), also occurs in Glacier National Park but is much less common than rough-fruited fairy-bell. The berry of Hooker's fairy-bell has a pointed tip and smooth skin, and its leaves are sparsely hairy on the upper surface. Small mammals and grouse eat the berries of both species. Humans eat them, too, but most who try them consider them tasteless. Taxonomists previously placed both species in the genus *Disporum*. Rough-fruited fairy-bell is also known as wartberry fairy-bell.

FALSE SOLOMON'S-SEAL

Smilacina racemosa
Lily Family (Liliaceae)

Description: False Solomon's-seal is a perennial herb with arching, unbranched stems 8–28 inches tall that sprouts from rhizomes. The foliage is covered with short hair. Leaves are oval and 2–6 inches long. They have wavy edges and a base that sheaths the stem. Tiny, white flowers are congested into an erect, pyramid-shaped cluster 2–4 inches long at the branch tips. Each flower is composed of 6 tiny, petal-like tepals. In fruit, the plant produces a cluster of red berries, each about ¼ inch long. False Solomon's-seal blooms May to July.

Habitat: Common in moist mountain shrublands, forests and avalanche chutes.

Notes: The berries of false Solomon's-seal are considered edible but may cause digestive ailments if too many are consumed. The Blackfeet Indians applied a powder made from the roots of this plant to wounds. This plant is sometimes called *Maianthemum racemosum*.

STARRY FALSE SOLOMON'S-SEAL

Smilacina stellata
Lily Family (Liliaceae)

Description: Starry false Solomon's-seal is a robust perennial with tall, unbranched, arching stems 4–16 inches high. The stems often grow in a zigzag pattern toward the top. The plant's lance-shaped leaves are 1–4 inches long, hairy on the underside, and often folded down the center. Star-shaped, white flowers are arranged in loose clusters at the stem tips. Each flower is about ½ inch wide and composed of 6 narrow, petal-like tepals. In fruit this plant produces distinctive green berries just over ¼ inch long with dark stripes. As the berries age, the stripes converge. Starry false Solomon's-seal typically blooms in June.

Habitat: Moist mountain forests and shrublands; open woodlands and meadows from montane to subalpine; common under aspen.

Notes: The leaves of starry false Solomon's-seal are much narrower and its flowers much bigger than those of false Solomon's-seal (*S. racemosa*, see above). Native Americans ate the berries, which, in moderate quantities, may cause diarrhea. Some botanists call this plant *Maianthemum stellatum*.

TWISTED-STALK
Streptopus amplexifolius
Lily Family (Liliaceae)

Description: Twisted-stalk is a robust, erect perennial with stems 12–40 inches high growing from spreading rhizomes. The stem is often bent at each leaf node, giving it a zig-zag appearance. Twisted-stalk's leaves clasp the stem and are arranged in an alternate pattern. They are 1½–4 inches long and oval-shaped with pointed tips. Bell-shaped, yellowish white flowers hang singly or in pairs from bent stalks at the leaf axils. Each flower is composed of 6 petal-like tepals fused into a tube toward the base and reflexed at the tip. Fruit are red to yellow berries about ½ inch long. Twisted-stalk blooms in July.

Habitat: Common in moist mountain forests and shrublands from montane to lower subalpine; especially common along shady streams.

Notes: Flowers and fruit of twisted-stalk are easy to miss because they are often hidden below its leaves. This plant resembles false Solomon's-seal (*Smilacina racemosa*, previous page) and rough-fruited fairy-bell (*Prosartes trachycarpa*, pg. 79). Examine the flowers to tell the difference. Twisted-stalk produces flowers in the leaf axils, while false Solomon's-seal and fairy-bell produce flowers at branch tips.

FALSE ASPHODEL
Tofieldia occidentalis
Lily Family (Liliaceae)

Description: False asphodel, an erect perennial with a sticky stem, growing 4–16 inches tall. The plant is tufted, sprouting from short rhizomes. Its leaves are 1–10 inches long, linear and have a trough-like furrow running from base to tip. White, star-shaped flowers are arranged in a dense, terminal cluster. Each flower is just over ¼ inch wide with 6 narrow, petal-like tepals and 6 conspicuous purplish anthers surrounding a central ovary. The fruit is an egg-shaped capsule about ¼ inch long. False asphodel blooms in July and August.

Habitat: Fens, wet meadows and wet soil bordering streams, lakes and ponds; common in the subalpine and alpine zones; less common lower.

Notes: The rhizomes of false asphodel are edible. Some Native American tribes used them for food.

TRILLIUM
Trillium ovatum
Lily Family (Liliaceae)

Description: Trillium is a perennial herb with stems 4–16 inches tall sprouting from short rhizomes. A whorl of 3 leaves is produced near the top of the stem just below the flower. Each leaf is 1–5 inches long and broadly oval with a pointed tip. The solitary, stalked flower is composed of 3 showy, white petals (fading to pink with age), 3 green, narrow sepals and a central cluster of yellow stamens. Fruit is a yellowish green, oval capsule, 1–1½ inches long. Trillium blooms in May.

Habitat: Common in moist to wet, shady forests in the montane zone, almost always west of the Continental Divide.

Notes: This plant is sometimes called wake-robin. Trillium is one of the first flowers to bloom in the spring, emerging just after the snow melts in low-elevation forests. The common and genus name trillium is derived from the Latin word *tri*, referring to the plant's leaves, petals, sepals and stigmas, which occur in threes. Native Americans used trillium rhizomes to relieve childbirth pain.

BEARGRASS
Xerophyllum tenax
Lily Family (Liliaceae)

Description: Beargrass is a leafy perennial with erect flowering stems growing 1–4 feet tall. Its basal leaves, 6–24 inches long, grass-like and wiry, form large tussocks emerging from thick rhizomes. Stem leaves are also grass-like, but much smaller. White flowers are produced at the top of long, erect stalks. The flower cluster is hemispheric at first, then elongates as lower flowers bloom. Each flower is just under 1 inch wide, star-shaped and composed of 6 petal-like tepals. Flowers mature into globe-shaped seed capsules about ¼ inch long. Beargrass blooms June to August.

Habitat: Abundant on open slopes in the subalpine zone; common in open forests, avalanche chutes and meadows from montane to subalpine.

Notes: Periodically beargrass will produce a mass flowering display that blankets open slopes with white, leaving a forest of dead stems the following summer. The leaves of beargrass were woven into baskets and hats by some Native American tribes. Elk and bighorn sheep browse the flowers, sometimes nipping off the entire flower cluster. Individual plants live a long time and are resistant to fire.

SHOWY DEATH CAMAS
Zigadenus elegans
Lily Family (Liliaceae)

Description: Showy death camas is an herbaceous perennial with grayish green foliage. Erect stems grow 4–24 inches tall from oval bulbs. The leaves are mainly basal, 3–12 inches long, and grass-like. Stem leaves are also grass-like, but much smaller. Greenish white to yellowish white, stalked flowers are arranged in a loose, terminal spike. Flowers are about ¾ inch wide with 6 spoon-shaped, petal-like tepals. Each tepal has a small, dark green, heart-shaped gland near its base. In fruit, this plant produces an oblong, 3-lobed capsule ½–¾ inch long. Showy death camas blooms in July and August.

Habitat: Calcareous soil of rocky, exposed slopes and cliffs; moist to wet meadows; open mountain forests; common from the montane to alpine zones.

Notes: Showy death camas has the unusual ability to grow successfully in both wet meadows and dry, rocky, calcareous soil. A related species, common death camas (*Z. venenosus*), has smaller flowers that are more crowded in the inflorescence. It grows primarily in mountain grasslands. The roots of both species are considered very poisonous in small amounts and should never be ingested. Both species are called death camas because they often grow with blue camas (*Cammasia quamash*, pg. 198). Early Native Americans and settlers harvested blue camas bulbs late in the season when only the bulbs were present. Since the aboveground portion of the plant had withered, people sometimes mixed death camas bulbs with those of blue camas, with fatal results.

MOUNTAIN LADY'S-SLIPPER
Cypripedium montanum
Orchid Family (Orchidaceae)

Description: Mountain lady's-slipper is a perennial herb with glandular-hairy foliage and leafy stems 8–24 inches tall. The leaves are broadly lance-shaped, 2–6 inches long, and slightly pleated along the veins. They sheathe the stem at the leaf base. A green, leaf-like bract is produced just below each of the 1–3 flowers. Each flower has a large, white, slipper-shaped lower petal sometimes tinged with purple on the inner surface. The sepals and upper petals are brownish purple, narrow and spiralled. Mountain lady's-slipper blooms in June and July.

Habitat: Moist to dry mountain forests with well-developed soil; sometimes occurs in shallow, limestone-derived soil; an uncommon plant in Glacier National Park.

Notes: Most members of the Orchid family, including mountain lady's-slipper, have evolved with specialized reproductive structures to facilitate pollination. Mountain lady's-slipper has a modified, sterile anther positioned at the opening of the lower, pouch-like petal that attract insects with its brilliant color. The blossoms are also fragrant, drawing pollinators with their sweet scent. Sparrow's egg lady's-slipper (*C. passerinum*), a rare plant in Montana, also occurs in Glacier National Park. Its sepals are green and not twisted like those of mountain lady's-slipper. Sparrow's egg lady's-slipper grows in boggy soil between fens and surrounding forest.

RATTLESNAKE-PLANTAIN
Goodyera oblongifolia
Orchid Family (Orchidaceae)

Description: Rattlesnake-plantain is a perennial herb with mottled, evergreen leaves and an erect, leafless, flowering stem 6–16 inches long. Basal leaf rosettes sometimes form patches on the forest floor. Each leaf is broadly lance-shaped, about 1–3 inches long and dark green with white patches on the upper surface. Often a thick, white stripe runs down the leaf midrib from base to tip. Greenish white flowers form a slender cluster toward the top of the flowering stem. The flowers may be arranged spirally or on 1 side of the stem. The upper sepal and 2 upper petals of each flower unite into a hood-like structure that protrudes over a pouch-shaped, lower lip petal. Rattlesnake-plantain blooms in July and August.

Habitat: Abundant in shady, moist forests from montane to lower subalpine zones; often growing with pipsissewa (pg. 160) and common huckleberry (pg. 164).

Notes: Rattlesnake-plantain's common name comes from the resemblance of its leaves to rattlesnake skin. Early settlers used it to treat snakebites and other skin lesions.

WHITE BOG ORCHID
Plantanthera dilatata
Orchid Family (Orchidaceae)

Description: White bog orchid is an erect perennial with leafy stems growing 8–32 inches tall. The leaves are broadly lance-shaped, 1½–6 inches long and spirally arranged along the stem. They become smaller toward the top of the stem and sheathe the stem at the leaf base. The white, fragrant flowers are about ½ inch long, subtended by a leaf-like bract and arranged in a narrow, spike-like cluster. Each flower has 2 lateral sepals, a "hood" composed of 2 petals and 1 sepal, and a long (about ¼ inch) lower lip petal. The lip petal is broad at the base, tongue-like at the tip and has a long, slender, curved spur projecting downward. White bog orchid blooms June to August.

Habitat: Common in wet soil of fens, wet meadows and ditches and beside streams; montane to lower subalpine.

Notes: White bog orchid is Glacier's most common bog orchid. Look for this plant growing in wet ditches along Lake McDonald. A related species, slender bog orchid (*P. stricta*), is similar to white bog orchid, but its lip petal is not broad at the base. Instead, it is narrow and gradually tapers toward the tip. Additionally, the spur on the lip petal of slender bog orchid is sac-like.

ROUND-LEAVED BOG ORCHID
Plantanthera orbiculata
Orchid Family (Orchidaceae)

Description: Round-leaved bog orchid is a perennial herb with leafless stems 12–24 inches high. Two leaves, opposite each other, grow appressed to the ground. They are fleshy, oval and 2½–6 inches long. Greenish white flowers are arranged in a narrow array at the top of the stem, each subtended by a small, leaf-like bract. The flowers are quite large (about ¾ inch long) and have a typical orchid structure with 2 lateral sepals, a "hood" composed of 2 petals and 1 sepal, and a long (about ½ inch) lower lip. The lower lip is narrow and strap-shaped, with a slender spur projecting backward from its base. Round-leaved bog orchid blooms in July and August.

Habitat: Moist forests in the montane zone.

Notes: The large, paired, basal leaves make round-leaved bog orchid easy to identify, even without the presence of flowers. These plants have an interesting method for pollinating each other. When an insect lands on the lower lip petal to feast on the nectar within the spur, it triggers the release of pollen clusters that spring forward and stick to the insect's head. When the insect visits another bog orchid flower, it brushes against and delivers pollen to the stigma of this flower, successfully completing pollination.

LADIES' TRESSES
Spiranthes romanzoffiana
Orchid Family (Orchidaceae)

Description: Ladies' tresses is a small, perennial herb with erect stems 4–12 inches tall. Its leaves are narrowly lance-shaped, 2–5 inches long and arranged in an alternate pattern along the stem. The leaves become smaller toward the top of the stem. White, fragrant flowers form 2–4 dense, vertical rows that spiral up the top of the stem. Each flower is composed of an upper hood and a tongue-shaped lower lip petal just under ½ inch long. The tip of the lower lip is wavy and points downward. Ladies' tresses typically blooms in August.

Habitat: Uncommon in wet meadows and fens from montane to subalpine.

Notes: The neat rows of flowers are thought to resemble long, beautiful braids of hair, hence the common name ladies' tresses. This unique flower arrangement distinguishes ladies' tresses from all other orchids in Glacier National Park.

TUFTED PHLOX
Phlox caespitosa
Phlox Family (Polemoniaceae)

Description: Tufted phlox is a mat-forming perennial with glandular-hairy herbage and ascending stems up to ½ inch tall. Stiff, narrow, awl-shaped leaves are ¼–½ inch long and arranged opposite each other on branches. Branch tips bear clusters of 1–3 flowers. They are tubular, about ½ inch in diameter, with 5 flaring lobes. Tufted phlox typically blooms in June.

Habitat: Rocky soil of exposed slopes, grasslands and dry, open forest in the montane zone; an uncommon plant, mainly occurring west of the Continental Divide.

Notes: Two other species of phlox, both white-flowered, grow in Glacier National Park. Alyssum-leaved phlox (*P. alyssifolia*) has wider leaves with white margins. Moss phlox (also called carpet phlox, *P. hoodii*) has long, tangled hair, like cobwebs, growing from its leaf bases. Both species, uncommon in the park, form mats or cushions on exposed slopes and in grasslands from mid-elevation to above treeline east of the Continental Divide.

SULPHUR BUCKWHEAT
Eriogonum umbellatum
Buckwheat Family
(Polygonaceae)

Description: Sulphur buckwheat is a mat-forming perennial herb with leafless stems growing 4–16 inches high from a branched rootcrown. The leaves are mainly basal, lance-shaped and ½–1¼ inch long. They are green above and densely covered with white, wooly hair beneath. Cream-colored flowers are sometimes tinged with pink or yellow and are less than ¼ inch long with a tubular base. They are grouped into stalked clusters and bundled together at the base to form a round to flat-topped umbel. Leaf-like bracts subtend the umbels. Sulphur buckwheat typically flowers June to August.

Habitat: Dry, rocky soil of open forests and shrublands, meadows and rock outcrops.

Notes: Cushion buckwheat (also known as silver plant, *E. ovalifolium*) is similar to sulphur buckwheat but has solitary, tightly congested umbels without visible bracts and oval leaves that are densely white-wooly on both surfaces.

AMERICAN BISTORT
Polygonum bistortoides
Buckwheat Family (Polygonaceae)

Description: American bistort is a perennial herb with erect stems 6–20 inches tall that sprout from a bulb-like rhizome. The leaves are narrowly lance-shaped and 2–4 inches long, with a few of the stem leaves becoming smaller toward the top of the plant. Brownish stipules (papery bracts) sheathe the stem near leaf bases. The pinkish white flowers are clustered into a thimble-shaped, terminal spike ½–2 inches long. Each flower is less than ¼ inch long and broadly funnel-shaped with 5 lobes. American bistort blooms June to August.

Habitat: Common in open meadows and moist grasslands at upper elevations and in alpine turf.

Notes: Native Americans used American bistort root in stews, soups and bread. Modern-day herbalists treat a wide variety of ailments with the plant. The root has diuretic, antiseptic and astringent properties, and has been used to heal cholera, diarrhea and infections of the mouth and skin.

MOUNTAIN KNOTWEED
Polygonum douglasii
Buckwheat Family (Polygonaceae)

Description: Mountain knotweed is a slender annual with erect, branching stems 1½–12 inches tall. Linear to narrowly lance-shaped leaves are ¼–2 inches long, gradually becoming smaller toward the top of the plant. Stipules (papery bracts) sheathe the stem near the leaf base. There are a few small, pinkish white flowers in the axils of upper leaves. Seeds are contained within shiny, black, 3-sided achenes. Mountain knotweed blooms in July and August.

Habitat: Open forests and shrublands; meadows, grasslands and streambanks; common on recently disturbed soil; montane to subalpine zones.

Notes: Native Americans and other early herbalists used knotweeds to alleviate diarrhea and kidney problems. Native Americans collected the seeds then pounded and ground them into a flour-like substance for cooking. The generic name *Polygonum* comes from the Greek words *polys*, "many," and *gonu*, "knees," referring to the jointed nature of the plants' stems.

ALPINE BISTORT
Polygonum viviparum
Buckwheat Family (Polygonaceae)

Description: Alpine bistort has an erect, unbranched stem growing 2–10 inches tall from a bulb-like rhizome. The basal leaves have short petioles and are narrowly oblong in shape. The leaf blades are ¾–3 inches long. Stem leaves are shorter and attached directly to the stem. Unisexual, white to pinkish flowers are clustered in a narrow spike ¾–2½ inches long. The lower flowers are replaced by oval, purplish bulbs, which may eventually drop to form a new plant. Fruit are 3-sided, brown achenes. Alpine bistort blooms in July and August.

Habitat: Moist, alpine turf; often grows with mountain avens (pg. 145).

Notes: Some modern-day herbalists use alpine bistort in cooking to impart a nutty flavor to dishes. Medicinally it has been used as an astringent, antiseptic and diuretic.

SPRING BEAUTY
Claytonia lanceolata
Purslane Family
(Portulacaceae)

Description: Spring beauty is a slender, delicate, perennial herb with erect to prostrate stems 2–6 inches high. Only one pair of stem leaves and 1–3 basal leaves are produced. The basal leaves are lance-shaped and arise from an underground, marble-like corm. Stem leaves are broadly lance-shaped and ½–2½ inches long. Bowl-shaped flowers are white with delicate, pink veins. They are 5-petaled and about ½ inch wide, subtended by 2 small sepals. Seeds are borne within a capsule just under ¼ inch long. Spring beauty blooms May to July.

Habitat: Moist, shallow soil of mountain meadows, grasslands and open forests with sunny, warm aspects; moist subalpine meadows where snow accumulates.

Notes: True to its name, spring beauty is one of the first and most beautiful plants to appear after the snow melts. The fleshy roots (corms) of this plant were an important staple in the spring diets of Native Americans, eaten both raw and roasted. Grizzly bears and small mammals also enjoy the roots when other springtime food is scarce.

ALPINE ROCK JASMINE
Androsace chamaejasme
Primrose Family (Primulaceae)

Description: Alpine rock jasmine is a mat-forming perennial that grows 1–4 inches tall. Its herbage is covered with long, silky hair. Leaves are narrowly oblong and about ½ inch long, forming basal rosettes. Funnel-shaped flowers, about ¼ inch in diameter, flare into 5 lobes and are white with a yellow center. They are arranged in a congested, hemispheric umbel on stalks that arise from the stem tip. Alpine rock jasmine flowers June to August.

Habitat: Grasslands and rocky slopes along the eastern front, always on limestone substrates; montane to alpine zones.

Notes: Alpine rock jasmine has a distinctive scent much like that of tropical jasmine. A related species, northern rock jasmine (*A. septentrionalis*), is an annual growing in similar habitats within Glacier National Park. It has a more open flower cluster and is less showy.

BANEBERRY
Actea rubra
Buttercup Family (Ranunculaceae)

Description: Baneberry is an erect, perennial herb with branched, leafy stems growing 12–31 inches tall. Each leaf is divided 2–3 times into groups of 3 toothed (sometimes lobed) leaflets, each 1–5 inches long. The small, white flowers are arranged in a terminal cluster (raceme). Each flower has 5–10 tiny, white petals, numerous stamens and 3–5 white sepals that fall soon after the flower blooms. Its fruit are bright red (occasionally white), glossy berries with several seeds and a black spot on the end. Baneberry flowers in June and July.

Habitat: Moist mountain forests from montane to lower subalpine zones; occurs on both sides of the Continental Divide, but is more common on the west.

Notes: True to its name, all parts of baneberry are considered poisonous, causing nausea, vomiting and dizziness if ingested. Its poisonous compound acts by suppressing the vagus nerve. Eating large quantities of the plant can cause cardiac arrest. Watch children carefully around this plant, especially when it is in fruit, since the beautiful red berries can be irresistible. Despite its bad reputation, baneberry was considered sacred by some northern Native American tribes, who used it to treat coughs and colds when nothing else worked. Its strength, both as a medicine and toxin, was highly respected and treated with caution.

CUT-LEAVED ANEMONE
Anemone multifida
Buttercup Family (Ranunculaceae)

Description: Cut-leaved anemone is an herbaceous perennial with several stems growing 8–28 inches high. Its herbage is covered with long hair. Basal leaves are pinnately divided 2–3 times into groups of 3 oblong leaflets, each tapering toward the tip. A whorl of pinnately divided stem leaves occurs at mid-stem, below the flowers. Creamy-white to yellowish flowers (sometimes tinged with magenta), ½–¾ inch wide, are produced in June and July. The plant usually produces 2–4 flowers per stem. Each flower has a central ring of numerous yellow stamens. Flowers develop into a globe-shaped cluster of silky-hairy achenes about ½ inch in diameter.

Habitat: Common in open forest, shrublands and grasslands in the montane zone.

Notes: The Blackfeet used cut-leaved anemone to cure headaches. They cut and burned the ripe seed heads and inhaled the smoke. Teton anemone (*A. tetonensis*) is very similar to cut-leaved anemone, but is shorter (usually less than 8 inches tall) and has 1 flower per stem. Teton anemone typically grows in subalpine and alpine meadows.

WESTERN PASQUEFLOWER
Anemone occidentalis
Buttercup Family (Ranunculaceae)

Description: The foliage of western pasqueflower is covered with long hair. It is a perennial with stems 6–16 inches tall. Stem height increases with maturity. Leaves grow in a basal cluster and a whorl of 3 near mid-stem. They are deeply divided 2–3 times into small segments, each less than ¼ inch wide. A single flower at the stem top blooms June to August. Flowers have 5–7 white, petal-like sepals and are about 1 inch long. True petals are absent. Fruit are tiny achenes bearing long, feathery styles. The styles are reflexed down and clustered into soft, fluffy heads (inset).

Habitat: Common in moist, open sites in the subalpine zone.

Notes: Plants in this genus (*Anemone*) are considered poisonous due to the presence of a caustic alkaloid, anemonine. This compound causes irritation and inflammation. Western pasqueflower, also known as windflower, is called *Pulsatilla occidentalis* by some botanists.

GLOBEFLOWER
Trollius albiflorus
Buttercup Family (Ranunculaceae)

Description: Globeflower is a perennial herb with clumped, erect stems 6–16 inches tall. The leaves are 1½–3 inches wide, palmately divided into 5 toothed or lobed, ovate segments, and are arranged alternately along the stem. Five to seven petal-like sepals form a single, white, bowl-shaped flower ¾ inch across, with a ring of yellow stamens and a central cluster of 10–20 united ovaries. In fruit, a cluster of pods is formed, each about ½ inch high with a spreading tip. Globeflower blooms in July and August.

Habitat: Seeps and wet depressions in montane forests (especially spruce); wet meadows and along streams in subalpine and alpine zones; often blooming near melting snow.

Notes: Globeflower resembles many members of the *Anemone* genus, and both genera are members of the same plant family (Buttercup). Globeflowers produce pod-like follicles in fruit, while *Anemones* form clusters of 1-seeded, fuzzy achenes. Globeflower is considered poisonous.

BUCKBRUSH
Ceanothus velutinus
Buckthorn Family (Rhamnaceae)

Description: Buckbrush is an erect, evergreen shrub growing 5–6 feet tall with green twigs and fragrant foliage. The oval leaves are shiny above, hairy below, and 1–3 inches long. Three prominent veins run from the base toward the tip and leaves are arranged alternately along branches. Clusters of numerous tiny, white, star-shaped flowers are produced at the tips of lower branches in June and July. They are less than ¼ inch wide with 5 hood-shaped petals. Fruit are tiny, glandular-sticky, 3-lobed capsules. Each lobe bears a low ridge on its back.

Habitat: Common in relatively open forests and along roads and trails from montane to subalpine.

Notes: Buckbrush produces thousands of fire-resistant seeds that can survive in soil for hundreds of years. The seeds depend on fire for germination. When a wildfire or pre-scribed burn opens the forest canopy and triggers germination, buckbrush plants readily colonize the area. The flowers, which make a soapy lather with warm water, can be used to cleanse the hair and skin. Herbalists use infusions of the leaves to treat a variety of ailments, incuding tonsilitis, lymph node and adenoid inflammation and ovarian and breast cysts. Buckbrush is also believed to reduce anxiety and internal bleeding.

SERVICEBERRY
Amelanchier alnifolia
Rose Family (Rosaceae)

Description: Serviceberry is a deciduous shrub with several erect stems up to 13 feet tall. The broadly oblong leaves are ¾–2 inches long, toothed on the upper half and rounded at the tip. Loose clusters of white flowers are produced at branch tips. They have 5 narrow, spatula-shaped petals, each about ½ inch long. Fruits are purple, fleshy, berry-like pomes ¼–½ inch wide. Serviceberry blooms April to July.

Habitat: Abundant in grasslands, shrublands, and moist to dry forests; often forming thickets in disturbed soil of montane grasslands.

Notes: One of our most common shrubs, serviceberry grows tall and scraggly under the forest canopy or short and dense in open grasslands. It is also known as saskatoon and juneberry. The juicy fruits are an important food source for bears, birds and other wildlife. Native Americans used them in pemmican, a dried cake of meat and fruit. Early settlers also used the fruit for food. The berries are a little seedy, but sweet and tasty and definitely worth trying. The Blackfeet Indians used them to treat digestive problems. They relieved eye and ear pain with eyedrops and eardrops made from boiled berries.

BLACK HAWTHORN
Crataegus douglasii
Rose Family (Rosaceae)

Description: Black hawthorn is a deciduous shrub or small tree growing up to 13 feet tall. Its branches bear large, straight thorns ½–1 inch long. The elliptic leaves are 1–2½ inches long and toothed along their margins, especially toward the tip. Clusters of white, 5-petaled flowers are arranged at branch tips. They are about ½ inch wide, bowl-shaped and bloom in June and July. Fruit are purplish black, smooth, berry-like pomes, each about ½ inch in diameter.

Habitat: Open forests, shrublands and grasslands in the montane zone; often along streams or marshes.

Notes: Black hawthorn fruit are an important food source for birds and other wildlife. Native Americans also collected the fruit for food and used the wood for tools. As the only tall shrub with such long, sharp thorns, the plant is easily identified in Glacier National Park.

WHITE MOUNTAIN AVENS
Dryas octopetala
Rose Family (Rosaceae)

Description: White mountain avens is an evergreen perennial with trailing, woody stems that often form mats. Its leaves are lance-shaped, leathery and ½–1 inch long. Solitary, saucer-shaped flowers are produced on stalks 1–3½ inches high. Flowers have 8–10 white petals, a central cluster of yellow stamens, and are ¾–1¼ inches in diameter. Clusters of seeds bear long, feathery styles. This plant blooms June to August.

Habitat: Abundant on rocky, exposed slopes and ridges above treeline; prefers calcareous substrates; less common in subalpine grasslands and moist turf.

Notes: White mountain avens is our most common alpine plant, forming mats that carpet alpine ridges. On some slopes, white mountain avens forms extensive stair-step patterns under the influence of wind and snow. Its low growth form enables it to retain moisture and warmth in extremely harsh conditions. Dryas flowers can act as little reflectors. Flies often spend the night in the flowers, which warm up soon after the sun rises.

WILD STRAWBERRY
Fragaria virginiana
Rose Family (Rosaceae)

Description: Wild strawberry is an herbaceous perennial with stems 1¼–6 inches tall. It spreads by stolons (runners). The leaves are divided into 3 toothed leaflets, each ½–2 inches long. The apical tooth on each leaflet is shorter than the adjacent teeth, and the leaves are blue-green in color. Clusters of several white flowers are produced in an open inflorescence. They are 5-petaled, saucer-shaped and about ¾ inch wide. A red, juicy, berry-like fruit is produced in late summer and early fall.

Habitat: Meadows, grasslands, shrublands and forests from montane to subalpine.

Notes: The fruits of wild strawberry arc an important food source for birds and small mammals. Native Americans also collected the fruit for food and used the roots to treat digestive ailments. A similar species, woodland strawberry (*F. vesca*), also abounds in Glacier National Park. Both species grow in similar habitats. The upper surface of woodland strawberry leaves have prominent veins, and the apical tooth on its leaflets is longer than the adjacent teeth.

OCEAN-SPRAY
Holodiscus discolor
Rose Family (Rosaceae)

Description: Ocean-spray is a deciduous shrub 3–10 feet tall with erect, arching branches. The leaves are 1½–3½ inches long, ovate and hairy with shallowly toothed and lobed margins. Sprays of small, white, saucer-shaped flowers produced in July and August form an erect or arching, pyramidal inflorescence at the branch tips. Each flower is about ¼ inch wide. In fruit, this plant produces tiny, hairy achenes.

Habitat: Dry, open forests and shrublands in the montane zone; more common west of the Continental Divide.

Notes: The flower clusters of ocean-spray resemble the foamy spray produced by ocean waves breaking against a rocky coastline. Native Americans used the tough wood of this plant for a multitude of tools, including arrows, bows and digging sticks. Some tribes made tea from the roots and used the fruit as food.

NINEBARK
Physocarpus malvaceus
Rose Family (Rosaceae)

Description: Ninebark is a deciduous shrub with erect, arching branches 3–7 feet tall and striped, gray bark. The leaves are 1–3 inches long and covered with star-shaped hairs. They are ovate in outline with 3 distinct lobes and toothed margins, similar to maple leaves. Clusters of white, saucer-shaped flowers are grouped in rounded clusters on branch tips. Each flower is about ½ inch wide and has a central cup-like disc called a hypanthium. In fruit, the plant produces a brittle, fuzzy capsule about ¼ inch long. Ninebark typically flowers May to July.

Habitat: Dry shrubland or woodland slopes with sunny exposures; common around West Glacier and on south-facing slopes along the Middle Fork Flathead River.

Notes: This plant is also known as mallow ninebark. The common name ninebark refers to the many layers of shredding, peeling bark that characterize the plant. The generic name *Physocarpus* comes from the Greek word *phyton,* "bladder" and the Latin word *karpon,* "fruit," referring to the slightly inflated fruit this plant produces in late summer. Rooted easily from cuttings, ninebark appears as an ornamental shrub in many northwest native-plant gardens.

CHOKECHERRY
Prunus virginiana
Rose Family (Rosaceae)

Description: Chokecherry is a deciduous shrub up to 17 feet tall with purplish gray bark. The toothed leaves are 1½–4 inches long, elliptic in outline, and pointed at the tip. There are 2–3 distinct glands on the leaf stalk (petiole) just below the blade. A cylindrical cluster of white flowers is produced May to July. Each flower is saucer-shaped, 5-petaled and about ½ inch wide. Fruit are red cherries, becoming dark with age. They are about ½ inch in diameter and hang downward in clusters.

Habitat: Shrubby thickets in the montane zone; often occurring along streams, bordering grasslands and in avalanche chutes.

Notes: The sour fruit of chokecherry was mixed with meat by Native Americans to make pemmican. Chockecherry jam, wine and syrup have been popular for centuries and are still made today. The flesh of chokecherries is edible, but the pit contains a very toxic substance (hydrocyanic acid). Ingesting a large amount is potentially fatal, especially to children. A related species, bitter cherry (*P. emarginata*), is also common in Glacier National Park. Its flower clusters are hemispheric instead of cylindrical, and its leaves are rounded at the tip instead of tapering to a point.

WILD RED RASPBERRY
Rubus idaeus
Rose Family (Rosaceae)

Description: Wild red raspberry is a deciduous shrub with erect to lax, prickly stems growing ½–5 feet tall. The leaves are palmately divided into 3–5 toothed, lance-shaped leaflets, each 1–3 inches long. One to four white flowers are produced from upper leaf axils in June and July. Flowers are about ½ inch wide with 5 slender petals and 5 glandular, reflexed sepals. The fruit are small, red and hemispheric, shaped like a typical raspberry. They are about ½ inch in diameter.

Habitat: Common on rock slides, burned slopes and on rocky stream banks from montane to lower subalpine.

Notes: Wild red raspberries are edible and have been used in wine, syrup and tea. Some herbalists use a tea made from the leaves to ease menstruation and childbirth. However, it can irritate the digestive tract if too much is taken internally. Black raspberry (*R. leucodermis*), with hooked spines along its branches, grows on the west side of Glacier National Park around Lake McDonald.

THIMBLEBERRY
Rubus parviflorus
Rose Family (Rosaceae)

Description: Thimbleberry is a deciduous shrub growing 1½–5 feet tall with shredding bark. The leaves are shaped like maple leaves, with 3–7 pointed lobes. They are 2–6 inches long and bristly-hairy on both sides. Several white, 5-petaled flowers are usually grouped in an open cluster on stem tips. They are saucer-shaped and 1–2 inches wide, blooming in June and July. Thimbleberry's fruit are dome-shaped and raspberry-like, ½–¾ inch wide and often sparsely hairy.

Habitat: Abundant in moist forests, shrublands and avalanche chutes from montane to subalpine zones.

Notes: The fruits of thimbleberry are juicy and quite tasty. Native Americans used them as food and they are popular "trail snacks" for modern-day hikers. Some Native American tribes also used the leaves to line containers and as toilet paper.

DEWBERRY
Rubus pubescens
Rose Family (Rosaceae)

Description: Dewberry has long, trailing stems and short, erect shoots 1–8 inches high. Leaves are pinnately divided into 3 toothed, ovate leaflets 1–3 inches long. They arise in clusters of 2–4 from the erect shoots. Flowers grow from the stem tips or directly from the main, trailing stem. Each flower is composed of five white petals, about ¼ inch long. Red, globe-shaped fruit are sometimes produced at stem tips and are about ½ inch in diameter. Dewberry blooms in June and July.

Habitat: Common along the edge of fens and marshes and in wet spruce forests in the montane zone; primarily occurs west of the Continental Divide.

Notes: A similar species, dwarf raspberry (also known as nagoonberry, *R. pedatus*), also produces trailing stems that hug the ground in wet areas. Dwarf raspberry leaves are usually palmately divided into either 5 leaflets or 3 leaflets with the lateral ones deeply lobed. The plant grows in spruce forest and on stream terraces in the McDonald and Waterton Valleys. Look for it along the trail from Goat Haunt to Kootenai Lakes.

WESTERN MOUNTAIN ASH
Sorbus scopulina
Rose Family (Rosaceae)

Description: Western mountain ash is a tall, deciduous shrub with erect to spreading branches up to 10 feet tall. Twigs are often white-hairy. Leaves are pinnately divided into 9–13 narrowly lance-shaped, toothed leaflets, each 1–3 inches long and pointed at the tip. Dense clusters of 70–200 tiny, white flowers are produced in a flat-topped infloresence. Orange to red, berry-like fruit are tightly clustered and about ¼ inch long. Western mountain ash flowers in June and July.

Habitat: Moist subalpine forests, slopes and avalanche chutes; less common in moist, montane sites.

Notes: Sitka mountain ash (*S. sitchensis*) also grows in Glacier National Park but is less common. Its twigs are red-hairy and its leaflets are rounded at the tip. Western mountain ash often grows with beargrass (*Xerophyllum tenax*, pg. 82) and common huckleberry (*Vaccinium membranaceum*, pg. 164). Grosbeaks, waxwings and grouse relish the fruit of both sitka and western mountain ash.

BIRCH-LEAVED SPIRAEA
Spiraea betulifolia
Rose Family (Rosaceae)

Description: Birch-leaved spiraea is a deciduous shrub sprouting from spreading rhizomes, with stems 8–32 inches tall. The ovate leaves are toothed toward the tip and 1–3½ inches long. Tiny, white, cup-shaped flowers are densely grouped into flat-topped clusters 1–3 inches wide. Each flower is just under ¼ inch wide with 5 petals and 25–50 long stamens. In fruit, a cluster of 5 cylindrical capsules less than ¼ inch long forms for every fertilized flower. This plant blooms in July and August.

Habitat: Abundant in moist to dry forests, on shrubby slopes, adjacent to grasslands and in avalanche chutes; montane to subalpine zones.

Notes: A similar species, subalpine spiraea (*S. densiflora*), is common in the subalpine zone. It has pink flowers and its leaves are hairy along the margins. Deer and elk browse the twigs of both species of spiraea. One of the most common shrubs in Glacier, birch-leaved spiraea is abundant along hiking trails all over the park.

NORTHERN BEDSTRAW
Galium boreale
Madder Family (Rubiaceae)

Description: Northern bedstraw is an herbaceous, rhizomatous perennial with 4–sided, erect stems 4–20 inches tall. Strap-shaped leaves ½–1½ inches long are whorled in groups of 4 along the stem. Tiny, white, 4-petaled flowers form branched clusters that arise from the axils of upper leaves. Each flower is less than ¼ inch wide. Two small nutlets form when the plant sets fruit, each less than ¼ inch long and covered with short hair. Northern bedstraw blooms June to August.

Habitat: Well-drained soil of meadows, grasslands and open forest from montane to subalpine.

Notes: Native Americans used the roots of northern bedstraw to make red and yellow dye. A related species, sweet-scented bedstraw (*G. triflorum*), is common in moist mountain forests. It has whorls of 6 strap-shaped leaves and prickly stems. Herbalists have used bedstraws to reduce inflammation and stop bleeding.

ROUND-LEAVED ALUMROOT
Heuchera cylindrica
Saxifrage Family (Saxifragaceae)

Description: Round-leaved alumroot is a perennial herb with slender stems 8–24 inches high. The upper portion of the flowering stem is glandular and slightly hairy. Leaves are primarily basal, heart-shaped in outline and 6–16 inches wide. Each leaf is palmately divided into 5–7 shallow lobes. Short-stalked, cup-shaped, white flowers are clustered in a narrow, spike-like arrangement (panicle) on stem tips. They are less than ½ inch long with inconspicuous petals and 5 rounded, petal-like sepals. Round-leaved alumroot blooms June to August.
Habitat: Common in the montane zone in shallow soil of rock outcrops, talus slopes and sparsely vegetated grasslands.
Notes: Native Americans boiled the roots of round-leaved alumroot into a tea for digestive problems. They also used it to relieve mouth and throat sores. The Blackfoot Indians used a mixture of dried root and buffalo fat to treat saddle sores on horses.

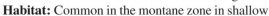

PRAIRIE STAR
Lithophragma parviflorum
Saxifrage Family (Saxifragaceae)

Description: Prairie star is a slender perennial with glandular-hairy stems 4–12 inches tall. Its leaves are primarily basal, round in outline and ½–1¼ inches wide. Each leaf is palmately divided into 3–5 deeply lobed segments. The lower surface is covered with a sparse layer of white hair. White, star-like flowers sometimes tinged with pink or purple are produced in loose clusters (racemes) of 3–11 at stem tips. Each flower is composed of 5 delicate petals that are ¼–½ inch long and 3-lobed. Prairie star blooms in June and July.
Habitat: Grasslands, meadows and open forest in the montane zone.
Notes: Prairie star is one of the most common and beautiful wildflowers blooming in the spring in pristine grasslands. Its basal leaves wither shortly after flowering, and by midsummer little evidence of the plant remains. Look for this plant in the expansive grasslands on the eastern side of Glacier National Park.

FRINGED GRASS-OF-PARNASSUS
Parnassia fimbriata
Saxifrage Family (Saxifragaceae)

Description: Fringed grass-of-Parnassus is a slender perennial with solitary flowers on stems 4–16 inches tall. Leaves are mostly basal, although a single, clasping leaf is often present midway up the stem. Leaves are broadly kidney- to heart-shaped, ½–2 inches wide and shiny. White, 5-petaled flowers are about ¾ inch in diameter. The petals are fringed toward the base along both sides. Just inside the petals of each flower, five anther-bearing stamens alternate with 5 fringed scales (staminodia). This plant blooms late, often in late August or even September.

Habitat: Common in wet soil along streams and fens and in wet meadows at all elevations; also common in wet meadows from subalpine to alpine.

Notes: There are 3 other species of grass-of-Parnassus in Glacier National Park. Fringed grass-of-Parnassus is the most common and conspicuous. The common and generic name Parnassus comes from a mountain in Greece where this plant was first discovered in the first century A.D. The specific name *fimbriata* means "fringed" in Latin.

SPOTTED SAXIFRAGE
Saxifraga bronchialis
Saxifrage Family (Saxifragaceae)

Description: Spotted saxifrage is a mat-forming, evergreen perennial with prickly leaves and slender stems 2–6 inches tall. Its needle-like leaves are ¼–½ inch long, spine-tipped, and clustered around the plant base. They are not deciduous and will remain intact for many years before drying and crumbling away. Flowers are 5-petaled, saucer-shaped and about ½ inch in diameter. Each white petal is spotted with purple. Flowers are arranged in loose clusters at stem tips, blooming in July and August.

Habitat: Abundant in dry meadows and turf, and on rocky slopes and cliffs from montane to alpine zones.

Notes: The spine-tipped leaves of spotted saxifrage set this species apart from the other 12 species of saxifrage in Glacier National Park. This hardy plant has been propagated by native gardeners and makes a beautiful addition to rock gardens in the cool climate of the northwest. It forms small, attractive mounds and large mats. The specific name *bronchialis* means "throat-like" or "throated" in Latin, referring to the appearance of the corolla tube. See the notes for western saxifrage on page 110 for a definition of the generic name. Look for this plant on the cliffs and rocky slopes lining the Highline Trail, near Logan Pass.

RED-STEMMED SAXIFRAGE
Saxifraga lyallii
Saxifrage Family (Saxifragaceae)

Description: Red-stemmed saxifrage is a perennial herb forming loose mats from spreading rhizomes. Its slender stems are reddish and 3–10 inches tall. Leaves are primarily basal. They are fan-shaped and ½–1½ inches long with toothed margins along the upper half. Several white, 5-petaled flowers are displayed in an open, branched infloresence at the top of stems. Each flower is about ¼ inch wide, blooming in July and August.

Habitat: Abundant on rock outcrops and in gravelly, moist soil of alpine meadows; often found along streams.

Notes: Red-stemmed saxifrage is our most common alpine saxifrage. Several high-elevation saxifrages such as brook saxifrage (*S. odontoloma*) and Merten's saxifrage (*S. mertensiana*) share similar characteristics, and all are reported to hybridize with one another. The leaves of brook saxifrage and Merten's saxifrage are nearly round in outline instead of fan-shaped like red-stemmed saxifrage leaves. Alaska saxifrage (*S. ferruginea*) also resembles red-stemmed saxifrage, but has a densely glandular inflorescense. Some lower flowers of Alaska saxifrage and Merten's saxifrage are replaced by tiny plantlets (miniature plants) that eventually drop off to form new plants.

WESTERN SAXIFRAGE
Saxifraga occidentalis
Saxifrage Family (Saxifragaceae)

Description: Western saxifrage is a perennial herb with a rosette of basal leaves and reddish, glandular stems 4–10 inches tall. Its leaves are ½–1½ inches long, elliptic in outline and have toothed margins. They often have a coat of reddish hair on the underside. Flowers are clustered in a dense, narrow arrangement that expands when the plant forms fruit. Each flower is just under ¼ inch wide and has 5 white petals and 5 reflexed sepals. Petals are dotted with a few yellow spots. Western saxifrage blooms May to August.

Habitat: Common in vernally moist soil of rock outcrops, meadows and grasslands at all elevations.

Notes: There are 13 species of saxifrage in Glacier National Park. Many are difficult to differentiate and may require a hand lens and technical plant key to identify with confidence. The generic and common name saxifrage comes from the Latin words *saxum,* "rock" and *frango,* "to break." By growing in rock crevasses, these plants give the illusion of splitting rock.

FOAMFLOWER
Tiarella trifoliata
Saxifrage Family (Saxifragaceae)

Description: Foamflower is a delicate perennial with erect stems that are slightly glandular toward the top. Stems are 8–20 inches tall. Leaves are spade-shaped and 1–3 inches wide. They have 3–5 main lobes and toothed margins, similar to maple leaves. Tiny, white flowers nod in a loose array at the top of the stem. Each flower is about ¼ inch wide and is composed of 5 thread-like petals, 5 oval sepals and 10 long, exserted stamens. In fruit, this plant produces oval capsules that split into a pair of scoop-like sections. Foamflower blooms June to August.

Habitat: Abundant in shady, moist mountain forests, especially west of the Continental Divide; look for carpets of foamflower in cedar-hemlock forests along Lake McDonald.

Notes: Foamflower's common name refers to the frothy appearance these plants have in large colonies when they all flower at once. The genus name *Tiarella* comes from the Latin word *tiara* and refers to the crown-like appearance of the fruit.

PARROT'S-BEAK
Pedicularis contorta
Figwort Family (Scrophulariaceae)

Description: Parrot's-beak is an herbaceous perennial with erect, slender stems growing 6–12 inches high. Its leaves are mostly basal, 1–6 inches long and pinnately lobed into narrowly oblong, toothed segments. Its white to cream flowers are loosely clustered in a terminal spike, subtended by deeply lobed, leaf-like bracts. Each flower is about ½ inch long and strongly 2-lipped, resembling a parrot's beak. The upper lip is elongated into a twisted, hood-like semicircle. The lower lip is short and broad. It blooms June to August.

Habitat: Subalpine and alpine meadows and grasslands; less common in montane grasslands and open forest.

Notes: Plants in the genus *Pedicularis* are parasitic on neighboring plants. They obtain some of their nutrients, water and carbon by tapping into and drawing food from their neighbor's roots. The particular neighboring species isn't important, and a single plant can form a parasitic relationship with several different plants.

SITKA VALERIAN
Valeriana sitchensis
Valerian Family (Valerianaceae)

Description: Sitka valerian is a perennial herb growing 12–28 inches tall. Its leaves are arranged opposite each other along the stem and are pinnately divided into 3–9 oval segments. The leaflets range in length from 2–3 inches, with the largest leaflet at the tip. Leaflets are ½–1½ inches wide and usually have toothed edges. Flowers are arranged in a hemispheric, terminal cluster. They are white (sometimes tinged with pink), about ¼ inch long and have 5 spreading lobes with 3 protruding stamens. Sitka valerian blooms in July and August.

Habitat: Abundant in moist meadows, open woodlands and on avalanche slopes in the subalpine zone; occurs higher and lower, but less frequently.

Notes: Northern valerian (*V. dioica*) is also common in Glacier National Park but usually occurs in drier forests at lower elevations than sitka valerian. Northern valerian has smaller flowers (about ¼ inch long), and the lateral lobes of its stem leaves are usually narrower (less than ¾ inch wide). Native Americans used cooked valerian roots to treat stomach aches, though they're considered poisonous when raw. A tea made from the roots has been used as a remedy for insomnia.

YELLOW ANGELICA
Angelica dawsonii
Parsley Family (Apiaceae)

Description: Yellow angelica is a slender perennial with stems 8–28 inches tall from a simple or branched rootcrown. Its leaves are twice pinnately divided into lance-shaped leaflets. Leaflets are finely toothed and 1–2 inches long. Yellow flowers are borne in a single compound umbel, a two-tiered flowering structure resembling an umbrella. Occasionally more than one umbel per plant may develop. There is a ring of lance-shaped, toothed bracts at the base of the umbel where it meets the stem. Fruits are flattened, smooth and broadly elliptic in outline. They are about ¼ inch long and have several longitudinal wings. Yellow angelica blooms in July and August.

Habitat: Common in meadows and open forest in the montane and subalpine zones; often grows with beargrass (pg. 82).

Notes: Glacier National Park is one of the few places where you can see yellow angelica; it occurs ónly here and in adjacent areas of Canada and north Idaho. The generic and common name *Angelica* is derived from the Greek *angelos,* "angel," referring to the plant's "angelic virtues" in medicine. Plants in this genus have been used for centuries to treat digestive problems, nausea, intestinal cramps and disorders of the female reproductive system, including menstrual discomfort.

AMERICAN THOROUGHWAX
Bupleurum americanum
Parsley Family (Apiaceae)

Description: American thoroughwax is a small plant (less than a foot tall) with narrow, lance-shaped, entire-margined leaves. Tiny, yellow flowers are clustered into a flat-topped, compound umbel. Small, leaf-like bracts occur at the base of each flower cluster and at the base of the main cluster. The oblong fruits bear raised ribs and are less than ¼ inch long. American thoroughwax blooms June to August.

Habitat: Common in dry, stony soil of exposed ridges and grasslands; montane to alpine.

Notes: The foliage of American thoroughwax has a rubbery, waxy texture. This plant is the only member of the Parsley family with undivided leaves in Glacier National Park. The generic name *Bupleurum* comes from the Greek words *bous,* "ox" and *pleuron,* "side," referring to abdominal swelling that occurs in cattle after eating the leaves of plants in this genus.

FERN-LEAVED DESERT PARSLEY
Lomatium dissectum
Parsley Family (Apiaceae)

Description: Fern-leaved desert parsley is a robust plant growing 1–3½ feet high with hollow stems. Its finely dissected leaves appear fern-like. Tiny, yellow flowers are clustered in compound umbels. The fruits are large (¼–½ inch long), oval in outline, flattened and bear two rib-like marginal wings. Fern-leaved desert parsley blooms in May and June.

Habitat: Dry meadows and open woodlands in the montane zone; almost always associated with very stony soil.

Notes: The distinguishing characteristic of fern-leaved desert parsley is its long, robust, fern-like leaves. Many Native American tribes used the starchy roots of this plant and other species of desert parsley for food. Mule deer eat the young shoots. A related species, Sandberg's desert parsley (*L. sandbergii*), also has finely dissected leaves but is much smaller (up to 10 inches tall) and grows at high elevations. Grizzlies eat the tuberous roots of Sandberg's desert parsley.

NINE-LEAVED DESERT PARSLEY
Lomatium triternatum
Parsley Family (Apiaceae)

Description: Nine-leaved desert parsley is a slender plant growing 7–16 inches tall from a taproot. The leaves are 2–3 times divided into linear segments up to ½ inch long. The tiny, yellow flowers are clustered in flat-topped umbels. The fruits are large (¼–½ inch long), narrowly elliptic in outline, flattened and have two marginal wings. Nine-leaved desert parsley blooms in June and July.

Habitat: Meadows, grasslands and open montane forests.

Notes: Blackfeet Indians used the roots of nine-leaved desert parsley as a cold remedy. The starchy roots of this plant are a favorite forage for small mammals and grizzly bears. Its foliage blends in with the grasses it associates with.

WESTERN SWEET CICELY
Osmorhiza occidentalis
Parsley Family (Apiaceae)

Description: Western sweet cicely is a robust perennial herb growing 1–3 feet tall. It has a distinctive anise-like odor when the foliage is crushed. The leaves are twice divided into nine lance-shaped leaflets. Each leaflet is 1–3 inches long and toothed or lobed along the margin. The light yellow flowers are tightly congested into umbels. The green fruits turn black when mature. They are linear, smooth and ½–¾ inch long. Western sweet cicely blooms in July and August.

Habitat: Moist aspen forests and avalanche sites from montane to subalpine; also common in open forests and along streams.

Notes: Western sweet cicely has been used in cooking to impart a sweet, anise-like flavor. A related species, mountain sweet cicely (*O. chilensis*, pg. 52), is distinguished from western sweet cicely by its white flowers and hairy fruit.

YELLOW FALSE DANDELION
Agoseris glauca
Sunflower Family (Asteraceae)

Description: Yellow false dandelion is a taprooted perennial growing 4–28 inches tall. Its leaves are narrowly lance-shaped, 1–14 inches long, somewhat hairy and sometimes shallowly toothed along the margins. All leaves grow from the plant base. Tiny, yellow flowers are arranged in a tightly clustered flower head resembling a dandelion. Several overlapping rows of hairy bracts surround each flower head. Sometimes these bracts are dotted with purple. In fruit, this plant produces slender, club-shaped achenes tipped with a tuft of white bristles. Yellow false dandelion blooms in July and August.

Habitat: Common in mountain meadows, along streams and on open slopes in the subalpine and alpine zones.

Notes: Both types of false dandelion (see orange false dandelion, *A. aurantiaca*, pg. 47) have milky sap that contains rubber-like compounds. When a portion of the leaf or stem is torn from the plant, this sap oozes from the cut end. Native Americans used various parts of agoseris plants to relieve inflamation and treat skin lesions. The leaves and flowers are edible and are sometimes used in salads.

HEART-LEAF ARNICA
Arnica cordifolia
Sunflower Family (Asteraceae)

Description: Heart-leaf arnica is a sparsely hairy perennial herb growing 6–20 inches tall from spreading rhizomes. Heart-shaped leaves grow opposite each other on the stem and in basal clusters. Leaves are 1–5 inches long, with the largest pair at the base. Flowering stems usually bear a solitary, showy, yellow flower head 1–2½ inches in diameter. Sometimes a pair of flower heads arises from the axils of the uppermost leaves. The flower head is composed of bright yellow ray flowers around the perimeter and darker yellow disc flowers clustered in the center of each head. Seeds are borne within achenes on the flower heads and are covered with hairy bristles on the apex. Heart-leaf arnica blooms June to August.

Habitat: Abundant in dry to moist forests from montane to subalpine zones; sometimes forms a loose carpet of leaves in the forest understory.

Notes: Arnicas have been used medicinally as a remedy for swelling and bruising. However, taken internally, these plants can severely irritate the digestive system. Contact with open wounds may allow toxins to enter the bloodstream, resulting in skin ulcers or other problems; medicinal use is best left to experts. A related species, mountain arnica (*A. latifolia*), looks much like heart-leaf arnica. The two can be distinguished by looking at the leaves. The middle stem leaves of mountain arnica are largest, and the leaves are usually not heart-shaped.

LONG-LEAVED ARNICA
Arnica longifolia
Sunflower Family (Asteraceae)

Description: Long-leaved arnica usually forms clumps of stems 12–28 inches tall, sprouting from creeping rhizomes. The foliage is short-hairy and glandular. Lance-shaped leaves grow opposite each other, with 5–7 pairs usually produced per flowering stem. Leaves have entire margins, are 2–6 inches long and lack petioles. Several yellow flower heads are grouped at the top of the stem, each 1–2 inches in diameter. Heads consist of a central cluster of disk flowers surrounded by 8–13 ray flowers. Long-leaved arnica blooms in July and August.

Habitat: Wet, stony soil in the subalpine zone; near or east of the Continental Divide.

Notes: Despite their cheerful appearance, arnicas are considered poisonous when taken internally, causing blistering of the digestive tract.

HAIRY ARNICA
Arnica mollis
Sunflower Family (Asteraceae)

Description: The stems of hairy arnica grow 8–16 inches tall, sprouting along spreading rhizomes. They are often separated from clusters of basal leaves growing along the same rhizome. The foliage is hairy and glandular. Leaves grow opposite each other in 2–4 pairs along the stem. They are lance-shaped to elliptic in outline, 1–4 inches long and have tiny teeth along the margin. The lowest pair are stalked (petiolate). Flower heads are produced singly or in clusters of 2–3 at the top of stems. Each head is about 2 inches in diameter with 12–18 ray flowers surrounding a button of tightly clustered disk flowers. Hairy arnica blooms June to August.

Habitat: Common in moist subalpine meadows, open forest and along streams; less common in the montane and alpine zones.

Notes: Herbalists make an external liniment from arnica leaves to relieve pain from sprains, bruises and breaks. However, it is considered toxic if it enters the bloodstream and should never be used if the skin is broken. Some species of arnica are hard to separate because they are thought to hybridize with one another. A hand lens and technical plant key is often necessary for a confident identification.

RYDBERG'S ARNICA
Arnica rydbergii
Sunflower Family (Asteraceae)

Description: Rydberg's arnica is a low-grow-ing perennial with glandular-hairy foliage. Flowering stems are often separate from the clusters of basal leaves and usually bear a soli-tary yellow flower head. Occasionally 2–3 flower heads are produced per plant. Its leaves are elliptic to lance-shaped in outline, about 2 inches long, and may be toothless or slightly toothed along the margins. Three to four leaf pairs are produced along the erect stem, but only the basal leaves have petioles (stalks). Flowers are produced in densely clustered, broadly conical flower heads at the top of stems. A central button of dark yellow disk flowers is surrounded by 7–10 yellow ray flowers, each about ¾ inch long. Rydberg's arnica blooms in July and August.

Habitat: Stony, shallow soil of subalpine and alpine meadows and slopes; common near and east of the Continental Divide.

Notes: Another common high-elevation arnica found in Glacier National Park is alpine arnica (*A. alpina*). Alpine arnica has long, wooly hair covering its foliage, an adaptation that helps it survive in exposed alpine environments.

TWIN ARNICA
Arnica sororia
Sunflower Family (Asteraceae)

Description: Twin arnica is a slender perennial with narrowly lance-shaped leaves that grow in a basal cluster and in pairs along the stem. The leaf bases are sometimes slightly hairy. Solitary (some-times 2–3) yellow flower heads are produced at the top of stems. Each flower head is composed of a tightly clustered, central button of disk flowers surrounded by radiating, petal-like ray flowers. Twin arnica blooms in June and July.

Habitat: Common in dry, montane grasslands west of the Continental Divide; sparsely distributed east of the Divide.

Notes: Look for this plant in the extensive prairies along the western border of Glacier National Park near the North Fork of the Flathead River. The word arnica comes from the Greek *arnikis,* meaning "lamb's skin," referring to the soft texture of arnica leaves. The specific name *sororia* means "sisterly."

ARROWLEAF BALSAMROOT
Balsamorhiza sagittata
Sunflower Family (Asteraceae)

Description: Arrowleaf balsamroot is a perennial with a leafless stem, large taproot and silvery-hairy foliage. Its leaves are large (up to 12 inches long) and triangular in outline. Long flower stalks bear a large, single sunflower-like head, 2–4½ inches wide. Each head is composed of 13–21 bright yellow ray flowers that surround a central button of tightly clustered, dark yellow disk flowers. This plant is one of the largest and most showy spring plants, blooming in May and June.
Habitat: Common in montane grasslands.
Notes: The grasslands of Glacier National Park come alive with color in the spring due to brightly colored wildflowers such as arrowleaf balsamroot. Look for it in the western grasslands near the North Fork of the Flathead River. The Blackfeet Tribe used the roots of arrowleaf balsamroot for food. This plant also provides spring forage for elk, deer and bighorn sheep.

DANDELION HAWKSBEARD
Crepis runcinata
Sunflower Family (Asteraceae)

Description: Dandelion hawksbeard is a perennial herb up to 20 inches tall with milky sap. Leaves are mainly basal, but a few small leaves may be scattered along the stem in an alternate pattern. The plant's basal leaves are up to 4 inches long, elliptic in outline and sometimes bear backward-pointing teeth. One to twelve flower heads per plant are arranged loosely at the branch tips. Flower heads are 3–6 inches high and made up of 20–50 tightly clustered, yellow ray flowers, appearing somewhat dandelion-like. This plant blooms in June and July.
Habitat: Common in moist soil of open sites such as grasslands and meadows and near wetlands; montane to subalpine.
Notes: A high-elevation hawksbeard species, dwarf hawksbeard (*C. nana*), grows on exposed ridges and talus slopes. Dwarf hawksbeard produces leaves and yellow flower heads in a tufted, cushion-like arrangement, providing protection against cold, windy conditions.

BLANKETFLOWER
Gaillardia aristata
Sunflower Family (Asteraceae)

Description: Blanketflower is a perennial herb with rough-feeling foliage and stems growing up to 16 inches tall. A basal rosette of toothed or entire (toothless) leaves appears first. As the plant grows and matures, it produces lobed leaves in an alternate pattern along the stem. Leaves are lance-shaped in outline and up to 6 inches long. Large (about 2½ inches wide), showy flower heads are borne at the top of stems either singly or in loose groups of 2 or 3. Each flower head has a ring of yellow ray flowers around the perimeter and a central button of brownish purple disk flowers. Ray flowers are 3-lobed at the tip and may be tinged with purple at the base. Blanketflower blooms June to August.

Habitat: Common in montane meadows, grasslands and woodlands.

Notes: The colorful flowers of this plant are thought to resemble intricately dyed blankets made by some Native American tribes. Early herbalists used blanketflower to treat skin lesions and to alleviate cold symptoms. Because blanketflower tolerates drought relatively well, it has been domesticated and used extensively in landscaping where water is in short supply.

GOLDEN ASTER
Heterotheca villosa
Sunflower Family (Asteraceae)

Description: The foliage of golden aster is covered with long, erect, white hair, giving the plant a grayish green cast. Clusters of stems grow up to 20 inches tall from a taproot. Leaves are produced at the plant base and in an alternate pattern along the stem. The leaves are lance-shaped, ¾–2 inches long and have entire margins. A short, open, flat-topped cluster of several flower heads is produced at the top of flowering stems. Each flower head is about 1 inch in diameter and is made up of a central cluster of yellow disk flowers surrounded by 10–25 yellow ray flowers. Golden aster blooms in July and August.

Habitat: Common in well-drained soil of grasslands and woodlands; often occupies disturbed habitats such as roadsides, streambanks, or where soil has slumped on a steep slope.

Notes: Golden aster's soft, wooly foliage sets it apart from most other yellow-flowered, daisy-like plants that occupy similar habitats. This plant is also known by the Latin name *Chrysopsis villosa*.

WOOLY WEED
Hieracium scouleri
Sunflower Family (Asteraceae)

Description: Wooly weed is a robust perennial with milky sap and flowering stems growing up to 2½ feet tall. Its foliage is covered with long, stiff, white hair. Leaves are produced in a basal rosette and along the stem in an alternate arrangement. They are lance-shaped, up to 8 inches long and gradually get smaller toward the stem top. Several dandelion-like flower heads are loosely grouped in a branched arrangement at the top of the stem. Flower heads are made up of 15–50 tiny, tightly clustered yellow flowers. Wooly weed blooms in July and August.

Habitat: Common in well-drained soil of mountain meadows, grasslands and woodlands.

Notes: A similar species, narrow-leaved hawkweed (*H. umbellatum*), has hairless foliage and lacks a basal rosette of leaves. The milky white sap of wooly weed and other members of its genus (*Hieracium*) contains rubber-like compounds. Some Native Americans tore off leaves of these plants and chewed them like chewing gum. An exotic relative of wooly weed, meadow hawkweed (*H. caespitosum*), is on the increase in Glacier National Park. It closely resembles wooly weed but lacks stem leaves and typically grows in open, disturbed sites.

ALPINE GROUNDSEL
Senecio cymbalarioides
Sunflower Family (Asteraceae)

Description: Alpine groundsel is a small perennial growing up to 8 inches tall from short rootstocks. Its herbage is smooth and hairless. Leaves are up to 1½ inches long, oblong in outline and toothed along the margin. Lower leaves have long petioles (stalks), while upper leaves are usually stalkless and may be lobed along the margin. A single flower head or pair of flower heads is typically borne at the top of the stem. Flower heads are about ¼ inch high and composed of 7–11 yellow ray flowers surrounding a central button of tightly clustered yellow disk flowers. Ray flowers are ¼–½ inch long. Alpine groundsel blooms in July and August.

Habitat: Common in subalpine and alpine meadows with moist, rich soil.

Notes: The groundsel genus (*Senecio*) is one of the largest genera in Glacier National Park, with 13 documented species. Many of these are closely related, often making field determinations difficult. Alpine groundsel closely resembles another high-elevation groundsel species, dwarf mountain groundsel (*S. cymbalaria*), but their habitats differ. Dwarf mountain groundsel occupies sites with soil that is drier and has less organic matter. It is common on rocky slopes, outcrops and streambanks.

MORAINE GROUNDSEL

Senecio fremontii
Sunflower Family (Asteraceae)

Description: Moraine groundsel has sprawling stems up to 10 inches tall growing in tufts from a branched rootcrown. Its foliage is smooth and hairless. Thick leaves are ½–1¼ inches long and have scalloped edges. They are oval in outline and grow from the plant base and along the stem in an alternate pattern. The largest leaves grow at or near the middle of the stem. Several flower heads are borne at branch tips. Each flower head is ¼–½ inch high and is made up of several yellow ray flowers around the perimeter and a tight central cluster of yellow disk flowers. Ray flowers are ¼–½ inch long. Moraine groundsel blooms in July and August.

Habitat: Dry, well-drained soil of rocky meadows, moraine talus slopes and outcrops from subalpine to alpine.

Notes: The branches of the root crown of this species may be long and stringy, an adaptation for growing among the shifting substrate of moraine and rock slides. Some groundsel species contain compounds that are considered toxic in large quantities. One reference lists groundsels as carcinogenic.

LARGE-HEADED GROUNDSEL

Senecio megacephalus
Sunflower Family (Asteraceae)

Description: Large-headed groundsel is a robust perennial growing up to 27 inches high. Long, white hair partially covers its foliage, gradually thinning with maturity. The leaves are narrowly oval in outline and grow up to 8 inches long. They have finely toothed or toothless margins. Basal leaves have petioles (leaf stalks), while stem leaves are stalkless. Usually only one flower head is produced per stem. It is large (½–¾ inch high) and composed of a central button of yellow disk flowers surrounded by several yellow ray flowers, each about ½ inch long. This plant blooms June through August.

Habitat: Dry, rocky soil of open slopes and meadows; lower subalpine to alpine.

Notes: The large, solitary flower heads combined with tall stems distinguish this groundsel species from the other 12 growing in Glacier National Park. Another common name for plants in this genus is butterweed.

ARROW-LEAVED GROUNDSEL
Senecio triangularis
Sunflower Family (Asteraceae)

Description: Arrow-leaved groundsel is a robust, rhizomatous perennial growing up to 4 feet tall. Leafy stems bear flower heads at the top in a loose, flat-topped cluster. The large leaves (up to 6 inches long) are distinctly shaped like arrowheads and have toothed margins. They gradually get smaller toward the top of the stem. Two types of tiny, yellow flowers are clustered into flower heads just under 1 inch in diameter. Disk flowers are tightly grouped in the center of the flower head, while several ray flowers line the perimeter. Each ray is about ¼ inch long. Arrow-leaved groundsel blooms in July and August.

Habitat: Moist areas in open to partly shaded environments such as woodlands, meadows, avalanche slopes and along streams; primarily seen in montane to subalpine zones, but can occur higher.

Notes: There are 13 different species of groundsel (*Senecio* species) in Glacier National Park, many which are difficult to tell apart. The triangular leaves and lush growth form of arrow-leaved groundsel distinguish it from its relatives. This plant often forms dense, tall thickets in seeps and along streams. Butterflies are attracted to the thickets in late summer.

CANADA GOLDENROD
Solidago canadensis
Sunflower Family (Asteraceae)

Description: Canada goldenrod is a lush, herbaceous perennial growing 1–3 feet high from spreading rhizomes. Toothed, lance-shaped leaves are produced in an alternate pattern on the stem and are largest at or near mid-height. A loose cluster of numerous yellow flower heads is borne in a pyramidal arrangement at the top of the stem. Flower heads are approximately ¼ inch across and are composed of about 11–15 yellow ray flowers surrounding a central cluster of yellow disc flowers. Canada goldenrod blooms in July and August.

Habitat: Common in moist, relatively open sites in the montane zone; often seen in moist meadows, open forests and avalanche slopes.

Notes: Canada goldenrod is positively affected by moderate disturbance, often forming small thickets where the soil has been churned. A close relative of this plant, Missouri goldenrod (*S. missouriensis*), is similar to Canada goldenrod but typically smaller (up to 20 inches tall) and grows in drier habitats. Goldenrods (*Solidago* species) are a difficult group to differentiate. A technical plant key is often necessary.

NORTHERN GOLDENROD
Solidago multiradiata
Sunflower Family (Asteraceae)

Description: Northern goldenrod is a slender perennial with stems up to 16 inches tall and sparsely hairy foliage. Its oblong leaves are mostly basal and up to 6 inches long. Stem leaves become smaller toward the top. Long hair grows along the margins of the lower leaf petioles (leaf stalks). Several flower heads are arranged in a slender, oblong cluster at the top of the stem. Each flower head is approximately ½ inch in diameter and is composed of a central button of tiny, yellow disk flowers surrounded by about 13 yellow ray flowers. This plant blooms June to August.

Habitat: Open, dry grasslands, woodlands, shrublands and exposed, rocky slopes in the subalpine and alpine zones.

Notes: Northern goldenrod is one of the most common forbs in moist alpine turf. It has been used for centuries to treat intestinal maladies. Modern herbalists use this plant to treat cold symptoms and skin ulcers and as a hair rinse to add blond highlights.

HORNED DANDELION
Taraxacum ceratophorum
Sunflower Family (Asteraceae)

Description: Horned dandelion is a taprooted perennial with milky sap and smooth, hairless foliage. It closely resembles the weedy dandelion in lawns and flowerbeds. Flowering stems grow up to 6 inches tall. Oblong, large-toothed leaves up to 4 inches long form a basal rosette. Solitary flower heads are produced at the top of leafless stalks and are comprised of many tiny, tightly clustered ray flowers. Flower heads are bright yellow, 1½–2 inches wide and surrounded by 2 rows of tiny, leaf-like bracts (involucral bracts). The involucral bracts of the inner row are slightly swollen at the tip. This plant blooms in July and August.

Habitat: Moist, high-elevation meadows and slopes with rocky, sparsely vegetated soil.

Notes: Dandelions (*Taraxacum* species) are well known for their culinary application, especially for their use as salad greens. The entire plant is edible and high in many vitamins. It has been used by herbalists for tea, wine and beer. Medicinally dandelions have been used to treat digestive ailments, wrinkles, anemia and jaundice.

OREGON GRAPE
Berberis repens
Barberry Family (Berberidaceae)

Description: Oregon grape is a low, creeping shrub with stems 2–12 inches long. The leaves are arranged alternately along the stem and are divided into 5–7 spiny-toothed leaflets, similar to common holly leaves. These leaflets are green above (sometimes tinged with red or purple) and dull green with a whitish, powdery coating (bloom) below. Leaves are referred to as evergreen because they persist for two growing seasons, at the end of which they turn crimson and wither. The yellow, globe-shaped flowers are arranged in elongated clusters (racemes). Fruit are bluish purple berries about 2½ inches long. Oregon grape blooms in May and June.

Habitat: Montane forests and shrublands; less common in subalpine forests.

Notes: Another common name for this plant is barberry. Native Americans from various tribes used Oregon grape extensively for medicinal and ceremonial purposes. The Blackfeet used the bark and roots to treat kidney and stomach problems, as an antiseptic and to relieve itching. Modern-day herbalists consider Oregon grape a very valuable herb for its medicinal properties. It is used as a stimulant and mild laxative and as a remedy for anemia and general malnutrition. The berries of this plant are made into jam, jelly and wine.

YELLOWSTONE DRABA
Draba oligosperma
Mustard Family (Brassicaceae)

Description: Yellowstone draba is a low-growing perennial that forms small cushions to larger mats. Its flowering stems reach a maximum height of 8 inches. Dense tufts of narrowly oblong leaves are produced at the plant base. Each leaf is ¼–½ inch long and usually hairy, especially on the lower surface. A cluster of 2–8 yellow flowers is produced at the top of a leafless stem. Flowers are 4-petaled and less than ¼ inch long. In fruit, this plant has oval, hairy pods ¼–½ inch long. Yellowstone draba blooms in July and August.

Habitat: Common in high-elevation meadows and on cliffs and exposed slopes; usually found near or just east of the Continental Divide.

Notes: There are 14 species of draba in Glacier National Park, many of which are hard to differentiate. This species often flowers before the stem elongates, keeping its flowers close to the warmth of its basal leaf cluster. The warmer temperature increases the likelihood that insects will visit the flowers and that the plant will develop viable seeds. The generic and common name *Draba* means "acrid" in Greek, a characteristic of the genus according to one source. The specific name is derived from *oligo,* "few" and *sperma,* "seeded."

TWINPOD
Physaria didymocarpa
Mustard Family (Brassicaceae)

Description: Twinpod grows from a branched rootcrown, forming a tuft of grayish green leaves covered with appressed hair. Stems are typically 1–4 inches long and prostrate. Twinpod's leaves are primarily basal, with a few stem leaves growing in an alternate pattern. Basal leaves are spoon-shaped, ¾–2 inches long and often have shallow teeth along their margins. Stem leaves are much smaller and very narrow. Yellow flowers are produced in a loose, elongated cluster at the top of the stem. Each flower has 4 petals, each about ½ inch long. The fruit of this plant are inflated, 2-lobed pods ½–1¼ inches tall. The pods are usually wider than tall and are produced on spreading stalks. Twinpod blooms in May and June.

Habitat: Common in dry, sparsely vegetated soil of open sites in the montane zone; often seen on stream banks and open slopes.

Notes: The Blackfeet people used the juice of twinpod to treat sore throats and stomach ailments. The generic name *Physaria* is derived from the Greek word *physa,* or "bladder," referring to the inflated fruit. The specific name *didymocarpa* means "twin-fruited."

BRACTED HONEYSUCKLE
Lonicera involucrata
Honeysuckle Family (Caprifoliaceae)

Description: Bracted honeysuckle is a deciduous shrub with erect stems and branches 3–10 feet tall. The twigs are 4-sided. The shrub's leaves are oval in outline, 2–6 inches long, pointed at the tip and often broadest above the middle. The leaf underside is sparsely hairy and dotted with tiny glands. Pairs of pale yellow, tubular flowers hang from the leaf axils. Flowers are ½–¾ inch long and are subtended by 2 large purple bracts, each about ½ inch long. These bracts bend backward when the plant is in fruit. Its fruit are shiny, glandular, black berries just under ½ inch in diameter. Bracted honeysuckle blooms in June and July.

Habitat: Common in moist mountain forests, along streams and in avalanche chutes.

Notes: The berries of bracted honeysuckle are beautiful but considered inedible due to their bitter flavor. Some sources report these berries may be poisonous. They are, however, an important food source for bears, birds and other animals.

LANCE-LEAVED STONECROP
Sedum lanceolatum
Stonecrop Family (Crassulaceae)

Description: Lance-leaved stonecrop is a tufted perennial with fleshy, succulent foliage and stems growing up to 8 inches high. Its leaves are yellowish green and narrowly lance-shaped. They are round in cross section, ¼–¾ inch long and grow in an alternate pattern along the stem. Clusters of leaves may also form basal rosettes. Yellow flowers are produced at stem tops, arranged in dense, flat-topped clusters. Each flower has 5 petals and is about ¾ inch in diameter. In fruit, this plant forms long, pointed capsules that spread from a central point in a star-like formation.

Habitat: Stony soil of exposed ridges, rocky slopes, cliffs and sparse grasslands; common from montane to alpine zones.

Notes: A related species, narrow-petalled stonecrop (*S. stenopetalum*, inset) is quite similar but can be distinguished from lance-leaved stonecrop by the small plantlets it forms in the upper leaf axils. These plantlets may drop, take root and form new plants. Roseroot (*S. roseum*) grows in stony soil at high elevation. Roseroot has rose-colored flowers, oblong leaves and grows up to 4 inches tall. Native American tribes have used stonecrops (*Sedum* species) to treat a variety of ailments, ranging from skin ulcers to digestive problems. Rock gardners favor many domesticated stonecrop relatives.

SILVERBERRY
Elaeagnus commutata
Oleaster Family (Elaeagnaceae)

Description: Silverberry is a tall shrub (up to 13 feet high) with silvery gray foliage that often forms thickets from spreading rhizomes. Its oval leaves are 1–3 inches long and arranged in an alternate pattern along the stem. The leaves are silvery on the upper surface and covered with rust-colored scales on the underside. Small, light yellow flowers grow from leaf axils singly or in groups of 2 or 3. Each flower is funnel-shaped and about ½ inch long. Silvery, berry-like fruit are produced in the fall and are approximately ½ inch long. Silverberry blooms in June and July.

Habitat: Well-drained, rocky soil along streams and rivers, and on gravel bars and floodplains in the montane zone.

Notes: Silverberry gives off a distinctive, sweet aroma that can be detected many yards away from the plant. Members of the Blackfeet Tribe used the dried berries as ornamental jewelry. This shrub is called wolf willow in eastern Montana where it forms thickets along coulees too dry to support true willows. Look for thickets of this shrub near the foot of St. Mary Lake.

CANADA BUFFALOBERRY
Shepherdia canadensis
Oleaster Family (Elaeagnaceae)

Description: Canada buffaloberry is a tall shrub with erect, spreading branches up to 10 feet high. Its twigs are covered with rust-colored scales when young. The oval leaves are 1–3 inches long and arranged opposite each other along branches. Leaves are dark green and shiny above and fuzzy beneath with rust-colored scales. Tiny, yellow flowers are clustered in the axils of new leaves and are often hidden under the leaves. Clusters of bright reddish orange berries are produced in late summer. Each berry is less than ¼ inch long. Canada buffaloberry blooms in May and June.

Habitat: Open forests and shrublands from montane to lower subalpine; upper-elevation grasslands.

Notes: Native Americans used the berries of Canada buffaloberry for food, mixing them with buffalo meat to make pemmican or drying them in the form of cakes for use during the winter. The cakes were added to stews and puddings. By themselves the berries taste terrible, but aren't bad if enough sugar is added. The berries contain a soapy substance (saponin) which produces a froth similar to egg whites when beaten. Canada buffaloberry is also known as soapberry. The generic name *Shepherdia* honors W. Shepherd, a distinguished curator of the Liverpool Botanical Gardens.

LEAFY SPURGE
Euphorbia esula
Spurge Family (Euphorbiaceae)

Description: Leafy spurge is an exotic, perennial herb with milky sap and leafy, branching stems growing 8–31 inches tall. Its leaves are linear and strap-like in outline, ¾–2½ inches long and have toothless (entire) margins. Flowers are loosely arranged at the tops of stems in a flat-topped, umbrella-like cluster. Flowers appear greenish yellow due to a pair of yellowish, petal-like bracts that subtend each tiny flower. The flowers themselves are inconspicuous and lack petals. Leafy spurge blooms in June and July.

Habitat: Open sites such as grasslands and meadows; locally common in the prairies of the North Fork Flathead River valley, where it is displacing native prairie vegetation; also encroaching in grasslands near St. Mary Lake.

Notes: Leafy spurge is considered one of the most threatening weeds in Glacier National Park. This plant spreads rapidly by sending out roots in all directions, producing monocultures as it outcompetes native plants for water, nutrients and sunlight. Park staff are working hard to preserve Glacier's native vegetation and have initiated efforts to control the spread of weeds such as this one.

YELLOW SWEET-VETCH
Hedysarum sulphurescens
Pea Family (Fabaceae)

Description: Yellow sweet-vetch is a slender perennial growing 8–24 inches tall from a woody, branched rootcrown. Its dark green leaves are divided into 9–17 elliptic leaflets. Each leaflet is sparsely hairy and conspicuously veined on the underside. Pale yellow to cream-colored, pea-like flowers are produced in clusters of 20–100 on erect stalks. Flowers hang downward and are about ½ inch long. In fruit, this plant produces flattened pods that hang from stalks with 2–4 distinct constrictions between the seeds (loments). Yellow sweet-vetch blooms June to August.

Habitat: Mountain grasslands and open slopes with rocky, well-drained soil on the eastern side of Glacier National Park; high-elevation ridges, slopes and meadows near the Continental Divide.

Notes: Yellow sweet-vetch is a popular food source for bears in Glacier National Park. Look for places where bears have excavated the root of this plant along trails that meander through open slopes. Native Americans, trappers and early settlers also used the root of sweet-vetch for food. Two purple-flowered sweet-vetch species also occur in the park, but aren't as common. Alpine sweet-vetch (*H. alpinum*) and northern sweet-vetch (*H. boreale*) both grow in moist, open sites from montane to subalpine zones. The two species can be differentiated by looking at the leaflets. Alpine sweet-vetch has conspicuous veins on the underside of its leaflets and its leaflets are sparsely hairy, while the underside of northern sweet-vetch leaflets are obscurely veined, and the leaflets are usually quite hairy (especially on the lower surface). Sweet-vetches are often mistaken for milk-vetches (*Astragalus* species), but can be recognized by the constricted fruits and the conspicuous, squared-off keel petal of the flowers.

SWEET PEA
Lathyrus ochroleucus
Pea Family (Fabaceae)

Description: Sweet pea is a climbing, trailing perennial with stems up to 32 inches long. Its leaves are pinnately divided into 6–8 leaflets that are egg-shaped in outline. The terminal leaflet is replaced by a gripping tendril. Small, stalked clusters of 5–10 pale yellow flowers grow from the junction between leaf and stem (leaf axil). Each pea-like flower is about ½ inch long and composed of an upper banner petal, two lateral wing petals and two lower petals that are fused along the bottom edge. Seedpods are linear, slightly flattened and 1½–3 inches long. Sweet pea blooms in June and July.

Habitat: Moist, open, montane forests; common in aspen groves east of the Continental Divide.

Notes: Sweet pea seeds and pods were used as food by early Americans, but are only safe in small amounts. They contain neurotoxins that, in large quantities, can cause a loss of coordination and permanent paralysis.

YELLOW SWEET CLOVER
Melilotus officinalis
Pea Family (Fabaceae)

Description: Yellow sweet clover is a sweet-scented biennial with smooth, hairless foliage. Branched stems grow 20–40 inches tall. Leaves are divided into 3 oblong, toothed leaflets, each ½–1¼ inch long. Yellow flowers are produced in narrow arrays from upper leaf axils. Each flower is less than ¼ inch long and has a typical Pea family structure with an upper banner petal, two lateral wings, and a lower lip petal. The fruit of this plant is an oval pod, ¼ inch long, that contains a single seed. Yellow sweet clover blooms in July.

Habitat: Common along roads and other disturbed areas.

Notes: A white-flowered relative, white sweet clover (*M. alba*), is also common in Glacier National Park and grows in similar habitats. Like yellow sweet clover, it is an introduced species and thrives in recently disturbed soil.

SILKY LOCOWEED
Oxytropis sericea
Pea Family (Fabaceae)

Description: Silky locoweed is a perennial herb with long, silky hair covering its foliage. Flowering stems are 2–12 inches high. Its leaves, 4–10 inches long, are divided into 7–17 leaflets that are oblong in outline. Each leaflet is ½–1 inch long. Clusters of 6–25 yellow flowers are produced at the tops of leafless flowering stems. Each flower is ½–1 inch long and has a typical pea flower structure. Seedpods are erect and crowded together at the tops of flowering stems. Pods are about ¾ inch long, thick-walled and rigid. Silky locoweed blooms May to July.

Habitat: Open sites ranging from montane grasslands to alpine ridges and slopes.

Notes: A similar species, mountain crazyweed (*O. campestris*), grows in the same habitats and can be difficult to separate from silky locoweed unless mature pods are present. The pods of mountain crazyweed are thin-walled and yield to fingertip pressure when mature, whereas silky locoweed pods are stiff under pressure.

YELLOW CLOVER
Trifolium agrarium
Pea Family (Fabaceae)

Description: Yellow clover is an herbaceous annual, 6–16 inches tall, with erect or ascending stems. Stem leaves grow in an alternate pattern and are divided into 3 narrow, oblong leaflets. Each leaflet is ½–¾ inch long. Clusters of 30–100 yellow flowers are arranged in globe-shaped clusters at the tops of stems. Each flower is structured like a typical pea flower, with a banner, wings and keel, and is about ¼ inch long. Yellow clover blooms in July and August.

Habitat: Road shoulders and disturbed meadows in the montane zone; introduced from Europe; more common west of the Continental Divide.

Notes: All of the 5 clovers (*Trifolium* species) that occur in Glacier National Park are introduced weeds. Their spread is limited to open and disturbed sites so there is little concern for these species significantly altering Glacier's native plant communities. Red clover (*T. pratense*) is another common occupant of roadsides and disturbed areas. It has clusters of large (½–¾ inch long) reddish purple flowers. White clover (*T. repens*), with clusters of white flowers sometimes tinged with pink, grows in similar habitats.

WESTERN ST. JOHN'S-WORT
Hypericum formosum
St. John's-wort Family (Hypericaceae)

Description: Western St. John's-wort is a low-growing, rhizomatous perennial with stems up to 8 inches high. Elliptic leaves are ½–¾ inch long, dotted with black spots and arranged opposite each other along the stem. Yellow, 5-petaled flowers are about ¾ inch in diameter and are also dotted with black, especially along the petal margins. Clusters of 75–100 stamens are bundled in the center of each flower. Fruits are membranous capsules about ¼ inch long. Western St. John's-wort blooms in July and August.

Habitat: Moist, open sites at high elevation, such as wet, alpine meadows and along streams; often occurs in shallow soil.

Notes: A related species, common St. John's-wort (*H. perforatum*, also known as Klammath weed and goatweed), also grows in Glacier National Park and is an aggressive weed. Introduced from Europe, it spreads rapidly in open, disturbed soil and is especially common in old burns along the Middle Fork Flathead River. St. John's-worts contain compounds that have been shown to combat anxiety and mild to moderate depression. They are also potent antiviral agents and are currently being studied for use against AIDS. Look for western St. John's-wort in the meadows around Logan Pass. A dwarf, alpine form of this plant (variety *nortoniae*) is named for Gertrude Norton, who studied the botany of the Flathead region in the early twentieth century. Many people consider her to be Montana's first female botanist.

GLACIER LILY
Erythronium grandiflorum
Lily Family (Liliaceae)

Description: Glacier lily is a delicate perennial growing 4–16 inches high from a fleshy, bulb-like root (corm). Its foliage is smooth and hairless. The basal leaves are narrowly elliptic in outline and 4–8 inches long. They are somewhat fleshy and usually produced in pairs. Nodding, bright yellow flowers are produced singly or in clusters of 2–3. Each flower is about 1–2½ inches wide with 6 petal-like tepals curving backward from the flower center. In fruit, an erect, oval, 3-lobed capsule is produced. Glacier lily blooms from May to August.

Habitat: Abundant in open mountain forests and grasslands and in high-elevation meadows, appearing just after the snow melts.

Notes: Glacier lily is one of Glacier National Park's signature plants, creating fields of vibrant yellow on slopes and meadows in the spring. Its flowers bloom at low elevation early in the spring, moving higher as the high country loses its blanket of snow. Glacier lily roots are harvested and eaten by bears and rodents. Entire slopes sometimes appear rototilled due to bears digging up the nutritious roots. Native Americans also used them for food. On sunny days the petal-like tepals curve up to expose the 6 dangling stamens, but they hang down to cover the flower parts on cloudy days. In some plants the anthers are yellow, while in others they are red. A white-flowered form is common along the North Fork of the Flathead River.

YELLOW BELL
Fritillaria pudica
Lily Family (Liliaceae)

Description: Yellow bell is a small perennial herb with stems 4–10 inches tall growing from bulbs. Its leaves arise from the middle of the stem in pairs, or a few may be whorled around one point on the stem. Leaves are strap-shaped, 1–4 inches long and somewhat fleshy. Solitary (sometimes 2–3), yellow, nodding flowers are produced in May. They are composed of 6 petal-like tepals that overlap, giving the flower a bell-like appearance. Each flower is about ½–¾ inch long. In fruit, these plants produce erect, egg-shaped capsules, about ¾ inch long.

Habitat: Mountain meadows and grasslands; somewhat uncommon.

Notes: Tepals of yellow bell turn reddish brown as they age. They are one of the earliest blooming flowers to appear in dry grasslands and meadows. Several Native American tribes used yellow bell roots as food. They are an important food source for a variety of animals, including bears and small mammals.

YELLOW WATER-LILY
Nuphar luteum
Water-lily Family (Nymphaeaceae)

Description: Yellow water-lily is an aquatic perennial growing from robust, underwater rhizomes. Leaves are round to heart-shaped, 4–12 inches in diameter and float on the water surface (some are submerged). Large, floating, yellow flowers have 6–9 petal-like sepals and inconspicuous petals. Many reddish yellow stamens surround a distinctive, plate-like stigma. Seeds are contained within a ribbed, oblong capsule about 1½ inches long. Yellow water-lily blooms June to August.

Habitat: Occurs in a handful of small mountain lakes on the west side of Glacier National Park.

Notes: Native Americans ground the seeds of yellow water-lily into flour for use in baking. They harvested, ground and cooked the large, underwater rhizomes into porridge and soups. Look for this plant floating on the surface of Howe Lake, a short hike off the inside North Fork Road.

YELLOW BUCKWHEAT

Eriogonum flavum
Buckwheat Family (Polygonaceae)

Description: Yellow buckwheat is a cushion-forming, perennial herb with leafless, white-hairy stems growing 4–12 inches tall. Its leaves are oblong in outline, ¾–1½ inches long, green above and white-hairy beneath. Yellow, hairy, funnel-shaped flowers are grouped into several stalked clusters. These clusters are bundled together to form a hemispheric inflorescence (umbel). The umbel is subtended by a whorl of leaf-like bracts. Yellow buckwheat flowers June to August.

Habitat: Abundant in stony soil of dry meadows, exposed ridges, rock crevices and talus slopes from montane to alpine.

Notes: Buckwheat seeds are important food sources for small mammals. Many species of buckwheat have been incorporated into rock gardens in northern climates. Look for this plant on talus slopes above treeline along the Highline Trail and in the prairies along the North Fork of the Flathead River.

YELLOW COLUMBINE

Aquilegia flavescens
Buttercup Family (Ranunculaceae)

Description: Yellow columbine is a perennial herb with freely branching stems 8–28 inches high. The leaves are mainly basal and divided into wedge-shaped, lobed segments, each ½–1½ inches long. Loose clusters of large, yellow flowers are produced June to August, each with 5 spreading sepals and 5 smaller, tubular petals. The petals have a nectar-bearing spur that projects backward from the point of attachment. The fruit is a cluster of 5 glandular pods that open along the inner side.

Habitat: Meadows and woodlands from montane to lower alpine zones; along streams and on rocky slopes.

Notes: Columbines produce pockets of nectar in the small knob located at the closed end of each petal, attracting pollinators with long tongues like butterflies and hummingbirds. The leaves of this plant look like the leaves of meadow rue (*Thalictrum occidentale*, pg. 175), but the flowers of the two species are very different.

MOUNTAIN BUTTERCUP
Ranunculus eschscholtzii
Buttercup Family (Ranunculaceae)

Description: Mountain buttercup is a perennial herb with erect stems growing 3–10 inches tall. Most leaves arise from the base of the plant. They are about 1 inch long, wedge-shaped and divided into 3–5 lobed or toothed segments. There are often no stem leaves, but when present they are typically divided into 3 linear lobes. Yellow, 5-petaled, bowl-shaped flowers are ½–¾ inch wide and bloom June to August. Smooth, tiny, shiny achenes enclose each of the seeds. They have a straight, beak-like projection and are borne in hemispheric clusters.

Habitat: Abundant in moist, subalpine and alpine meadows where snow collects.

Notes: There are 18 different species of buttercup in Glacier National Park; mountain buttercup is our most common high-elevation species. A hand lens and technical plant key are often necessary to differentiate between many of these species.

LITTLE BUTTERCUP
Ranunculus uncinatus
Buttercup Family (Ranunculaceae)

Description: Little buttercup is a slender herb growing 10–30 inches tall. Basal leaf blades are 1–3 inches wide and divided into 3 lobed leaflets. Each leaflet is ovate in outline. Stem leaves are smaller with narrower lobes. The inconspicuous flowers are about ¼ inch wide with 5 bright yellow petals. Seed heads are globe-shaped and bear a cluster of 1-seeded achenes (fruit). The achenes are less than ¼ inch long and sparsely hairy with a curved, beak-like projection. The plant flowers in June and July.

Habitat: Moist, open forests and shrublands; often along streams or in other small openings where light filters through the forest canopy.

Notes: Little buttercup is one of the most common albeit inconspicuous buttercups in Glacier National Park. All buttercups have a tiny, nectar-bearing pocket at the base of each petal that attracts pollinators. This buttercup is common along trails because the little hooked fruits readily attach to fur or clothing. A related, weedy species, tall buttercup (*R. acris*, inset) has recently been spotted in Glacier National Park. It grows in moist mountain meadows, is up to 32 inches tall and has large flowers (about ½ inch in diameter). Tall buttercup is common near Polebridge, just outside the western boundary of the park.

YELLOW MOUNTAIN AVENS
Dryas drummondii
Rose Family (Rosaceae)

Description: Yellow mountain avens is a mat-forming perennial with evergreen leaves and woody, trailing stems. The leaves are elliptic in outline and leathery, with prominent veins on the upper surface and wooly, white hair underneath. They are ½–1 inch long long. Solitary, yellow flowers are produced on stalks 2–10 inches tall. They are saucer-shaped with 8–10 petals. In fruit, a cluster of seeds forms, each with a long, feathery style. The styles are twisted together at first but soon take on the appearance of loose cotton (inset). This plant blooms June to August.

Habitat: Gravel bars along montane rivers and streams; less common near treeline on stony slopes and ridges.

Notes: The feathery styles of avens help work the seeds into soil by curling when wet and straightening when dry. The flowers nod in bloom then straighten to point upward when in fruit. All species of *Dryas* have an affinity for calcareous substrates.

LARGE-LEAVED AVENS
Geum macrophyllum
Rose Family (Rosaceae)

Description: Large-leaved avens is a tall, slender perennial with moderately hairy stems up to 3 feet high. The leaf blades are up to 8 inches long and pinnately divided into many leaflets. The terminal leaflet, much larger than the others, is orbicular in outline. Five green, reflexed sepals just under ¼ inch long subtend each 5-petaled, yellow flower. The flowers are saucer-shaped, about ½ inch wide and arranged in a loose, terminal, flat-topped cluster (cyme). In fruit, a spherical cluster of tiny, burred seeds (achenes) is produced, about ½ inch in diameter.

Habitat: Moist forest openings, wet meadows, seeps and streambanks from montane to lower subalpine.

Notes: The globe-shaped, bristly seed clusters of large-leaved avens are designed to catch on the clothing or fur of passersby, dispersing the seeds long distances. The hooked bristles are actually persistent styles that remain attached after fertilization occurs.

SHRUBBY CINQUEFOIL
Pentaphylloides fruticosa
Rose Family (Rosaceae)

Description: Shrubby cinquefoil is an erect, spreading shrub with deciduous leaves and stems 4–40 inches tall. The leaves are covered with silky hair and pinnately divided into 5 narrowly lance-shaped leaflets, each about ½ inch long. Yellow, 5-petaled flowers arise from the upper leaf axils and are clustered in groups of 1–5. In fruit, this plant produces achenes, about ½ inch long, covered with long, silky hair. Shrubby cinquefoil blooms June to August.

Habitat: Wide range of habitats, from moist mountain meadows to dry, subalpine slopes; found at all elevations.

Notes: Shrubby cinquefoil has the ability to adapt to a wider variety of habitats than any other plant in Glacier National Park. The only plant communities that cannot support it are deep, wet, low-elevation forests and alpine meadows where snowmelt occurs late in the season. Because it is so adaptable, this plant has been used extensively in gardens across the northwest. It's sometimes called *Potentilla fruticosa*.

BLUE-LEAVED CINQUEFOIL
Potentilla diversifolia
Rose Family (Rosaceae)

Description: Blue-leaved cinquefoil is a slender perennial herb with erect stems 4–16 inches tall. The foliage is sparsely hairy. Leaf blades are palmately divided into 5–7 toothed leaflets and often have a blue-green cast. Stem leaves are typically smaller than basal ones. Yellow, saucer-shaped flowers are loosely clustered at the stem tips. Each flower is about ¾ inch wide with 5 heart-shaped petals. In fruit, a dense cluster of achenes is produced, tucked inside the sepals. Blue-leaved cinquefoil flowers in June and July.

Habitat: Moist meadows, grasslands, open shrublands and exposed ridges from montane to alpine.

Notes: A related species, graceful cinquefoil (*P. gracilis*), has hairier foliage. Graceful cinquefoil usually occurs in the montane zone. There are 16 different species of cinquefoil in Glacier National Park, many with similar characteristics. A technical plant key is necessary to differentiate many of these species.

STICKY CINQUEFOIL
Potentilla glandulosa
Rose Family (Rosaceae)

Description: Sticky cinquefoil is a perennial herb with glandular-sticky foliage and slender stems 4–20 inches tall. Its basal leaves are oblong in outline and pinnately divided into 5–9 ovate, toothed leaflets, each ½–1½ inches long. Upper stem leaves are smaller. Loose clusters of white to yellow flowers are arranged at stem tips. They are saucer-shaped and ½–¾ inch wide with 5 petals and 5 glandular sepals. In fruit, this plant forms a cluster of smooth achenes, each with a style attached to its side, below the midline. Sticky cinquefoil flowers in June and July.

Habitat: Open, rocky grasslands, slopes, shrublands and woodlands from montane to lower subalpine; exposed slopes and ridges in the subalpine and alpine zones.

Notes: Two varieties of sticky cinquefoil occur in Glacier National Park. The taller variety, *glandulosa*, is common at lower elevations. The *pseudorupestris* variety is typically less than 12 inches tall and occurs at high elevation. Another common cinquefoil in Glacier National Park is white cinquefoil (*P. arguta*). It is similar to sticky cinquefoil, but its flower cluster is stiff and erect instead of loose and open. White cinquefoil is typically a more robust plant than sticky cinquefoil and is found in deep soil of mountain grasslands.

SIBBALDIA
Sibbaldia procumbens
Rose Family (Rosaceae)

Description: Sibbaldia is a low, mat-forming perennial with prostrate stems and erect shoots up to about 3 inches tall. Leaves are mainly basal, sparsely hairy and divided into 3 ovate leaflets, resembling strawberry leaves. Each leaflet is ½–¾ inch long with a few shallow teeth toward the tip. Inconspicuous, saucer-shaped, yellow flowers are arranged in flat-topped clusters. They are composed of 5 long, pointed sepals that alternate with 5 shorter yellow petals (each just under ½ inch long). Sibbaldia blooms in July and August.

Habitat: Abundant in subalpine and alpine meadows and turf; often in rocky, sparsely vegetated soil where snow accumulates.

Notes: Sibbaldia readily colonizes disturbed sites. It is often found with mountain heather (*Phyllodoce* species), wood rush (*Luzula hitchcockii*) and Drummond's rush (*Juncus drummondii*). Look for sibbaldia in the alpine turf around Logan Pass. It has been planted around Logan Pass by park staff as part of the park's effort to revegetate areas that have been disturbed by construction and other improvement projects.

WESTERN YELLOW PAINTBRUSH
Castilleja occidentalis
Figwort Family (Scrophulariaceae)

Description: Western yellow paintbrush is an herbaceous perennial with long, silky-hairy foliage that is often slightly sticky. It grows 2–8 inches tall. Leaves, 1–2 inches long, are narrowly lance-shaped with toothless margins. They are arranged alternately along the stem. Pale yellow to white flowers are densely clustered at the top of the stem. The flowers are tube-shaped with a long, arching upper lip and a small lower lip. The upper lip is less than half as long as the flower tube. Each flower is subtended by a pale yellow (sometimes green) bract, covered with sticky hair and sometimes lobed at the tip. Western yellow paintbrush blooms in July and August.

Habitat: Common in moist soil of meadows, slopes and ridges near treeline.

Notes: There are 3 other species of yellow paintbrush in Glacier National Park, but only one, sulphur paintbrush (*C. sulphurea*), grows in high-elevation sites like western yellow paintbrush. To differentiate between the two, examine the calyx and corolla. The calyx of western yellow paintbrush is about as long as the corolla, whereas the calyx of sulphur paintbrush is longer than the corolla. To complicate matters, the two often inter-breed, producing plants with characteristics intermediate between the two species. Western yellow paintbrush also hybridizes with a red-colored paintbrush, alpine paint-brush (*C. rhexifolia*, pg. 50), forming colonies with varying amounts of purple and white in the inflorescence. Look for these colonies at Logan Pass.

BUTTER-AND-EGGS
Linaria vulgaris
Figwort Family (Scrophulariaceae)

Description: Butter-and-eggs is a slender perennial with erect stems 8–32 inches high, often spreading vigorously by underground stems. Its foliage has a bluish cast. Linear leaves are 1–1½ inches long, toothless and arranged alternately along the main stem. The yellow and orange flowers closely resemble common garden snapdragons. They are strongly 2-lipped with a conical spur at the base of the lower lip. The upper lip is erect and divided into 2 lobes. The orange lower lip is 3-lobed and fuzzy. Flowers are clustered in a dense, terminal spike (raceme). Butter-and-eggs blooms in July and August.

Habitat: Introduced from Europe, this weed is common in disturbed soil of mountain grasslands and meadows, especially near Many Glacier and St. Mary.

Notes: Many of Glacier National Park's native grasslands have been impacted by human activity over the last century. Often the most visible sign left by early settlers is weed invasion, as is the case with butter-and-eggs. This plant spreads rapidly and can easily displace native plants in open, sunny sites.

YELLOW MONKEYFLOWER
Mimulus guttatus
Figwort Family (Scrophulariaceae)

Description: Yellow monkeyflower has a highly variable growth form; it can be an annual or perennial depending on its habitat. Permanently moist sites allow this plant to establish as a perennial and grow quite large. Sites that are moist in the spring, then dry as summer progresses, support smaller, annual plants. Often spreading by runners (stolons), yellow monkeyflower has erect to lax stems growing 4–20 inches tall. Its leaves are ½–2 inches long, ovate in outline, coarsely toothed and bear 3–7 prominent veins running from the base toward the tip. The yellow flowers are strongly 2-lipped and resemble snapdragon flowers. They are ½–1½ inches long and dotted with tiny red spots. Yellow monkeyflower blooms in July and August.

Habitat: Common in wet soil and shallow water along streams and on wet cliffs from montane to lower subalpine zones.

Notes: Another yellow-colored monkeyflower, mountain monkeyflower (*M. tilingii*), is also common in Glacier National Park. Mountain monkeyflower is smaller (up to 8 inches tall) than yellow monkeyflower, has shorter leaves (up to ¾ inch long), and typically grows at high elevation. Its flowers are large compared to the rest of the plant.

BRACTED LOUSEWORT
Pedicularis bracteosa
Figwort Family (Scrophulariaceae)

Description: Bracted lousewort is a perennial herb with erect, leafy stems 10–28 inches tall. Leaves are ½–2 inches long and pinnately divided into narrow, toothed segments. Tube-shaped flowers are crowded in a dense terminal spike, subtended by green, leaf-like bracts. Flowers are pale yellow to wine-colored, ½–¾ inch long and strongly 2-lipped. The upper lip is long and arching, with a short beak at the tip. The lower lip is smaller and 3-lobed. This plant blooms June to August.

Habitat: Abundant in subalpine woodlands, shrublands and meadows; often grows with beargrass (pg. 82) and huckleberry (pg. 164) on open slopes; occurs at all elevations.

Notes: The leaves of bracted lousewort resemble fern fronds. Elk browse the flowering portion of this plant. The common name lousewort refers to an old superstition that livestock ingesting this plant would become infested with lice.

YELLOW PENSTEMON
Penstemon confertus
Figwort Family (Scrophulariaceae)

Description: Yellow penstemon is an herbaceous perennial with erect stems 4–20 inches tall. Its leaves grow from the base of the plant and in an opposite pattern along the stem. They are ½–4 inches long, narrowly oblong to lance-shaped and have smooth, toothless margins. Yellow to cream-colored, tubular flowers occur in 2–4 dense clusters above each other at the top of the stem. Each flower is about ½ inch long with a 2-lobed upper lip and a 3-lobed lower lip. Yellow penstemon blooms in June and July.

Habitat: Common in dry, rocky soil of lower-elevation mountain meadows and grasslands.

Notes: Yellow penstemon is Glacier's only penstemon with yellow flowers. The other 7 species have flowers ranging in color from blue to purple.

ROUND-LEAVED YELLOW VIOLET
Viola orbiculata
Violet Family (Violaceae)

Description: Round-leaved yellow violet lacks a true stem. It sprouts leaves and flower stalks directly from rooted runners (stolons). Its leaves are ¾–1½ inches wide and nearly orbicular in outline with a shallow notch at the base. Leaves lie pressed to the ground and remain green throughout the winter. Bright yellow flowers arise from erect or lax flowering stalks about 1 inch long. Flowers are 5-petaled and lined with purple near the throat. There is a sac-like spur at the base of the lowest petal. The style tip is distinctly hairy. Round-leaved yellow violet blooms April to July.

Habitat: Moist mountain forests; more common on the west side of Glacier National Park.

Notes: A related yellow-flowered species, stream violet (*V. glabella*), occupies habitats similar to those of round-leaved yellow violet. Stream violet is an erect, leafy plant with leaves that are distinctly pointed at the tip. Many species of violets produce underground flowers that self-pollinate and produce seeds without ever opening. The flowers of violets are edible. The fruits, seeds and rhizomes, however, are considered poisonous.

ROSY PUSSY-TOES
Antennaria rosea
Sunflower Family (Asteraceae)

Description: Rosy pussy-toes is a mat-forming perennial herb with flowering stems 4–12 inches tall. Clusters of leaves are often connected by runners (stolons). Basal leaves are oval and less than ¾ inch long. Stem leaves are smaller and narrower than basal leaves. Flowers are tightly clustered into flower heads and surrounded by papery, pinkish bracts. Several flower heads are usually arranged in a cluster at the top of the stem. Rosy pussy-toes blooms May to July.

Habitat: Common in moderately dry, often rocky soil of meadows, grasslands and woodlands in the montane zone.

Notes: The flower of this plant may look pink, but the color actually comes from pinkish bracts surrounding the flower head. The specific name *rosea* reflects this characteristic. In all species of pussy-toes, the male and female flowers are on separate plants. Male flower heads are smaller and more globe-shaped.

ENGELMANN'S ASTER
Aster engelmannii
Sunflower Family (Asteraceae)

Description: Engelmann's aster is a tall (1½–6 feet) perennial with ribbed, leafy stems. Its foliage is sometimes sparsely covered with hair and tiny glands. Stem leaves grow in an alternate arrangement and are largest at mid-stem. Leaves are lance-shaped in outline, 2–4 inches long and have entire (toothless) margins. Flower heads are arranged in a widely branched inflorescence at the top of the stem. Each flower head is composed of a tightly clustered, central button of yellow disk flowers surrounded by 8–13 mauve ray flowers. Engelmann's aster blooms July to September.

Habitat: Common in moist soil of mountain meadows, avalanche chutes, aspen groves and open, subalpine forests.

Notes: Asters and fleabanes (*Erigeron* species) are often hard to differentiate because their flower heads are similar. By examining the involucral bracts (small, green, leaf-like bracts) that surround each flower head, one can distinguish the two genera. The involucral bracts of asters appear to overlap in rows of different lengths, similar to shingles on a roof. The bracts of fleabanes overlap slightly, but appear to be approximately the same length, surrounding the flower head in 1 or 2 rows.

TWINFLOWER
Linnaea borealis
Honeysuckle Family (Caprifoliaceae)

Description: Twinflower is a trailing, evergreen herb with opposite leaves and delicate stems up to 3 inches tall. Its broad, oblong leaves are ½–¾ inch long and have a few teeth along the margin on the upper half. Two light pink, funnel-shaped flowers nod from the top of each flowering stem. These delicate flowers are about ½ inch long and are slightly hairy on the inner surface of the flower tube. Twinflower blooms in June and July.

Habitat: Cool, moist, shady forest from montane to lower subalpine; often accompanied by bead lily (pg. 78) and huckleberry (pg. 164) in the forest understory; occurs on both sides of the Continental Divide, but is more common to the west.

Notes: Twinflower often forms loose, low-growing mats on the forest floor. The genus name *Linnaea* pays tribute to Swedish botanist Carolus Linnaeus (1707-1778), who developed the method of naming plants and animals with a genus and species binomial (2 names). Twinflower is said to have been one of Linnaeus's favorite flowers.

SNOWBERRY
Symphoricarpos albus
Honeysuckle Family
(Caprifoliaceae)

Description: Snowberry is a deciduous shrub growing up to 3 feet high from spreading rootstalks. The twigs are hairless and smooth, and bear leaves arranged opposite each other. Leaves are 1–2 inches long and have even margins. Leaves on immature twigs may be shallowly lobed. The light pink flower petals are fused into a bell-shaped tube about ¼ inch long. Flowers are clustered at the ends of branches and in some leaf axils. Fruit are ivory-colored berries ¼–½ inch in diameter. Snowberry blooms June to August.

Habitat: Abundant in dry to moist forests and shrublands from montane to subalpine.

Notes: Snowberry is Glacier's only shrub with large, ivory-colored berries. The berries are intriguing but are considered poisonous by some sources and should not be eaten. Snowberry is common in the shade, but produces fewer flowers and fruit than if it receives more sun. A related species, western snowberry (*S. occidentalis*), is less common in Glacier National Park. It has hairy twigs and a bowl-shaped flower.

MOSS CAMPION
Silene acaulis
Pink Family (Caryophyllaceae)

Description: Moss campion is a high-elevation plant that forms cushions 2–10 inches in diameter. The bright green, linear leaves are all basal and ¼–½ inch long. Flowers are produced singly on stems but sometimes cover the entire plant when in full bloom. Each flower is about ¼ inch in diameter and has 5 pink petals, each notched into 2 lobes. Seeds are contained within capsules that open by 3 tiny slits to release seeds in the fall. Moss campion blooms June to August. **Habitat:** Rocky, alpine tundra and stony ridges and slopes above treeline.

Notes: One of Glacier's most common alpine plants, moss campion is hard to miss when in full bloom. It produces brilliant alpine displays and has been incorporated into many domestic rock gardens. Other alpine plants such as alpine bistort (pg. 90) often establish in the protected centers of moss campion mats.

MOUNTAIN LOVER
Paxistima myrsinites
Bittersweet Family (Celastraceae)

Description: Mountain lover is an evergreen shrub growing 8–31 inches tall with 4-sided, spreading branches. Its shiny, green, leathery leaves are sharply toothed, ½–1 inch long and arranged opposite each other along branches. Four-petaled, inconspicuous, dark red flowers are produced in leaf axils and are less than ¼ inch in diameter. Clusters of flowers sometimes occur at branch tips. The fruit of this plant is a white, fleshy, oval capsule embedded in the central portion of the flower. Mountain lover blooms in May and June.

Habitat: Common in forests and shrublands from montane to subalpine zones, where snow cover is present throughout the winter; occurs on both sides of the Continental Divide, but is more common to the west.

Notes: Native Americans used mountain lover for a variety of medicinal purposes. It has been used for pain, tuberculosis and inflammation. The phrase "Pa kissed Ma" is commonly used to remember the genus name (*Paxistima*).

KINNIKINNICK
Arctostaphylos uva-ursi
Heath Family (Ericaceae)

Description: Kinnikinnick is a low-growing, trailing shrub with branches reaching a maximum height of 6 inches. Its stems are usually covered with fine hair and sometimes feel slightly sticky. The oblong, shiny leaves are ½–1 inch long, evergreen and have a leathery texture. Pink flowers hang in clusters from the tips of branches and bloom in May and June. Each flower is urn-shaped and less than ¼ inch long. Green berries, ¼–½ inch long, are produced in summer and turn red in the fall.

Habitat: Abundant in relatively dry forests at all elevations, particularly those dominated by pine species, larch or Douglas fir; also occurs in shrublands and grasslands, and in stony soil above treeline.

Notes: Kinnikinnick berries are a popular food source for bears. Native Americans used the dried leaves in a tobacco mixture for smoking. Although the berries look appetizing, they are tasteless and mealy, and ingesting too many may cause constipation.This plant is also known as bearberry.

PIPSISSEWA
Chimaphila umbellata
Heath Family (Ericaceae)

Description: Pipsissewa is a low-growing, perennial herb with a woody base and whorled leaves. Stems are usually 4–10 inches high. Its shiny, evergreen leaves are narrowly lance-shaped in outline, tapered toward the base and have toothed margins. Five-petaled, nodding, light pink flowers are produced on long stalks at the top of the stem. Flowers are dish-shaped, waxy and about ½ inch in diameter. In fruit, seed-bearing capsules are produced in an erect, slender column at the top of the plant. It blooms in July and August.

Habitat: Common in the understory of moist, shady forests from montane to subalpine.

Notes: Native Americans dried the leaves of pipsissewa for use in tobacco mixtures. Outside Glacier National Park it has been harvested commercially to flavor a variety of soft drinks, beer and candy. Pipsissewa is also known as prince's pine.

SMALL BOG-LAUREL
Kalmia polifolia variety *microphylla*
Heath Family (Ericaceae)

Description: Small bog-laurel is a short shrub (up to 8 inches tall) with evergreen leaves. Its leaves are lance-shaped in outline, ½–1 inch long and rolled under around the margin. The upper surface of each leaf is shiny green, and the underside is grayish. Leaves are arranged opposite each other along the stem. Five-petaled, pink flowers are arranged in loose clusters at the tips of branches. The petals are united into a dish-shaped corolla about ½ inch in diameter. Seeds are enclosed in a 5-segmented capsule produced in the fall. Small-bog laurel blooms May to July.

Habitat: Wet, organic soil of montane fens and marshes; wet subalpine and alpine turf, especially around streams, seeps and ponds.

Notes: Laurels contain poisonous compounds and should not be ingested. Fatalities in cattle and horses have been reported after grazing on this plant. Its pollination mechanism employs spring-loaded stamens tucked in pockets located on the inside of each petal. When an insect (or curious observer) lightly touches the stamen, it pops up, sprinkling pollen on its unsuspecting visitor. Glossy bog-laurel (*K. polifolia* variety *polifolia*), a taller plant with longer leaves and larger flowers, is locally common around the edge of McGee Meadow. Some taxonomists classify these two plants as separate species (*K. microphylla* and *K. polifolia*).

FOOL'S HUCKLEBERRY
Menziesia ferruginea
Heath Family (Ericaceae)

Description: Fool's huckleberry is a tall shrub with arching branches and shredding bark, growing up to 7 feet high. The foliage is hairy, slightly sticky and gives off a distinctive skunky smell when crushed. Leaves are ¾–2½ inches long and narrowly elliptic in outline. They are finely toothed along the margin and broadest toward the tip. Pinkish peach (sometimes orange), urn-shaped flowers are produced in clusters at the base of new twigs. Hard capsules appear in the fall, each less than ½ inch in diameter. Fool's huckleberry blooms June to August.

Habitat: Abundant in the understory of montane and subalpine forests, especially under subalpine fir on north-facing slopes.

Notes: Fool's huckleberry resembles common huckleberry (pg. 164). Fool's huckleberry is usually much taller with thinner, more delicate leaves, and it produces hard capsules instead of edible berries. The skunky smell of fool's huckleberry foliage is probably the most obvious characteristic that distinguishes the two. Fool's huckleberry is considered poisonous, causing headaches, weakness, vomiting and even paralysis when consumed in large quantities.

PINK MOUNTAIN HEATHER
Phyllodoce empetriformis
Heath Family (Ericaceae)

Description: Pink mountain heather is a dwarf shrub with spreading branches growing 4–8 inches tall. The evergreen leaves are needle-like and less than ½ inch long. They are crowded along the branches in an alternate pattern. The rose-colored flowers are bell-shaped, about ¼ inch long, and they nod from long stalks at the ends of branches. The tips of flower petals curve back. Pink mountain heather blooms in July and August.

Habitat: Moist to wet meadows and woodlands in the alpine and subalpine zones; commonly associated with dwarf trees at treeline, where snow lies late into the growing season.

Notes: A close relative of pink mountain heather, yellow mountain heather (*P. glanduliflora*), grows in similar habitats. It has yellow flowers and spreading (versus recurved) petal lobes. The two often grow together in alpine turf, where they may interbreed to produce hybrid offspring with pink flowers.

PINK WINTERGREEN
Pyrola asarifolia
Heath Family (Ericaceae)

Description: Pink wintergreen is a rhizomatous perennial herb with a basal rosette of evergreen leaves and leafless flowering stems 4–10 inches tall. Its shiny leaves are leathery, elliptic to heart-shaped in outline and 1–3 inches long. Light pink, cup-shaped flowers are loosely arranged in an elongated column on the flowering stem. The flowers have 5 petals, each about ¼ inch long, and a curved style that projects outward from the center of the flower. Pink wintergreen blooms in June and July.

Habitat: Moist sites such as shady forests, streambanks and fens; montane to subalpine.

Notes: Plants in the genus *Pyrola* rely on soil fungus for nutrition in addition to the food they get through photosynthesis. In some cases the plant can become completely dependant on soil fungus, producing only a flowering stem. Green-flowered wintergreen (*P. chlorantha*) is very similar to pink wintergreen but has greenish white flowers, and its leaves are usually smaller (less than 1 inch long).

COMMON HUCKLEBERRY
Vaccinium membranaceum
Heath Family (Ericaceae)

Description: Common huckleberry is a deciduous shrub growing 1–3 feet high, sometimes forming dense thickets. Its broadly lance-shaped leaves are 1–2 inches long and finely toothed around their margins. Pink (sometimes yellowish green) urn-shaped flowers are produced singly on stalks from the leaf axils. Flowers are almost ¼ inch long. Juicy berries, ¼–½ inch wide, are produced in late summer. They are initially small, firm and green, becoming red as they ripen (pictured), then juicy and deep purple at maturity. Common huckleberry blooms in May and June. Berries usually ripen from late July to August, depending on elevation.

Habitat: Abundant in the understory of moist to dry forests from montane to subalpine zones; often occurs with beargrass (*Xerophyllum tenax*, pg. 82), forming open shrublands on slopes near treeline.

Notes: Common huckleberry is one of Glacier National Park's most popular plants, loved by both hikers and wildlife. The delicious berries are harvested commercially outside of the park. Bears are particularly dependent on this plant as a food source. Although the berry crop varies from year to year, plants produce the largest fruit when partially exposed to sunlight through openings in the forest canopy. This plant is also known as mountain huckleberry. A few berries eaten here and there are perfectly legal, but check with park staff for current regulations on picking a larger amount of huckleberries.

LOW HUCKLEBERRY
Vaccinium myrtillus
Heath Family (Ericaceae)

Description: Low huckleberry is a low-grow-ing, deciduous shrub with spreading, green, short-hairy twigs reaching a maximum height of 12 inches. Its leaves are less than ¼ inch long and finely toothed along the margin. Pinkish, urn-shaped flowers are produced in leaf axils along branches. Flowers are just under ¼ inch long. Berries are green and firm when first formed, gradually turning red, then dark blue at maturity. They are about ¼ inch in diameter. Low huckleberry typically blooms in June.

Habitat: Common in the understory of spruce-fir and lodgepole pine forests from mon-tane to subalpine; Glacier's most common low-growing species of huckleberry.

Notes: Low huckleberry is very similar to common huckleberry (previous page) but much smaller in stature. Another low-growing *Vaccinium* species, grouse whortleberry (*V. scoparium*), is even smaller (up to 8 inches tall), with leaves less than 1 inch long and tiny red berries.

BICKNELL'S GERANIUM
Geranium bicknellii
Geranium Family (Geraniaceae)

Description: Bicknell's geranium is an annual or perennial herb with branching, sprawling stems growing 4–20 inches high. Leaves are arranged opposite each other on the lower portion of the stem and alternately on the up-per portion. Each leaf is broadly heart-shaped in outline, 1–3 inches wide and cut into 5 in-dividual segments. These segments are then dissected even further into narrow lobes. Light pink to white, saucer-shaped flowers bloom in June and July. They are about 1½ inches wide and usually produced in pairs from the base of the upper leaves. Seeds are contained within cylindrical capsules about ¾ inch long, which split into 5 recurved segments.

Habitat: Disturbed, open sites in the montane zone; especially common after fire.

Notes: The seeds of Bicknell's geranium require abrasion or heat combined with expo-sure to germinate, which makes them especially suited to colonize after wildfires or prescribed burns. Seeds can remain in the soil for decades, waiting for the proper com-bination of environmental conditions.

STICKY GERANIUM
Geranium viscosissimum
Geranium Family (Geraniaceae)

Description: Sticky geranium is a perennial herb sprouting from a woody rootcrown with hairy, sticky herbage and stems 8–35 inches high. Leaves are mostly basal, 2–6 inches wide and divided into 5–7 lobes. Each lobe is sharply toothed along the leaf margin and pointed at the tip. The lower leaf surface is hairy only on the veins. Pinkish purple to magenta flowers are composed of 5 rounded petals, each ½–¾ inch long with delicate purple veins. Fruit are elongated, beaked capsules. Sticky geranium typically blooms in July and August.

Habitat: Montane grasslands, meadows and open forest.

Notes: Sticky geranium occasionally hybridizes with white geranium (*G. richardsonii*, pg. 75) to produce plants with characteristics of both species. These hybrids are produced where both species grow closely, as in the aspen parklands along the eastern edge of Glacier National Park. Herbalists tout its properties as an astringent and treatment for many ailments including diarrhea, gastritis, gout and bladder pains. The Blackfeet Tribe used its powdered roots to stop external bleeding and a tea made from the leaves to alleviate cold symptoms.

SWAMP CURRANT
Ribes lacustre
Gooseberry Family (Grossulariaceae)

Description: Swamp currant is a spiny, erect shrub growing 20–40 inches tall. Thorn pattern is variable, but typically there are large, stiff thorns at the branch nodes and bristly spines between nodes. Leaves are shiny above, hairless, ½–3 inches wide and shaped like maple leaves with 3–5 palmate lobes. Brownish pink, saucer-shaped flowers hang in drooping clusters, 7–15 per group. Each flower is about ½ inch wide. Fruit are black berries, about ¼ inch in diameter, with bristly-glandular hair. Swamp currant blooms May to July.

Habitat: Abundant in avalanche chutes, along streams and in the understory of moist to wet forests from montane to subalpine.

Notes: The fruit of swamp currant is edible, but most people find it tasteless. A similar species, wild gooseberry (*R. oxyacanthoides*), also occurs in Glacier National Park, but isn't as common as swamp currant. The flowers of wild gooseberry are bell- to funnel-shaped, its berries are smooth and hairless, and its leaves are slightly sticky to the touch. Northern currants have been used for centuries as food, alone or as an addition to pemmican and bread. Some native tribes viewed the entire plant as poisonous, using the branches to ward off evil spirits.

NODDING ONION
Allium cernuum
Lily Family (Liliaceae)

Description: Nodding onion is a slender perennial growing from small, oval bulbs, with a stem that arches at the tip. It grows 4–16 inches high and smells strongly of onion. Its slender, linear leaves arise from the plant base. They are about ¼ inch wide, u-shaped in cross section, and shorter than the flowering stem. The flowers are stalked and arranged in a nodding umbel. Each flower has 6 pinkish rose, petal-like tepals. The tepals are less than ¼ inch long, forming a cup-shaped flower with 6 protruding stamens. In fruit, a tiny capsule forms with 6 horn-like points at the tip. Nodding onion blooms June to August.

Habitat: Mountain grasslands, meadows and open forests; especially common in aspen groves.

Notes: The nodding stem and onion smell of this species are its most distinctive characteristics. In fruit, the arching stem of nodding onion becomes somewhat erect, which helps the plant disperse seeds. Native Americans collected and dried the bulbs for use as winter food. Eaten raw, they have an onion flavor that many find overwhelming, but cooking mellows this taste to a pleasant sweetness.

MOUNTAIN HOLLYHOCK
Iliamna rivularis
Mallow Family (Malvaceae)

Description: Mountain hollyhock is a robust perennial with leafy stems 1–7 feet tall. The leaves are 2–8 inches wide and maple-like with 5–7 lobes. Large (up to 1½ inch wide), pink to rose-colored flowers are produced in the axils of upper leaves. They form an elongated, dense, terminal inflorescence (raceme). Fruits are stiff-hairy, wheel-like capsules with several sections, similar to the sections of an orange. Mountain hollyhock blooms June to August.

Habitat: Moist, open sites experiencing disturbance, from montane to subalpine zones; often occurring along streams or roads.

Notes: Mountain hollyhock is one of the first plants to appear following a fire because the seeds germinate readily after heating or scouring. The flowers closely resemble larger, cultivated hollyhocks. Stiff hair covering the fruit sometimes causes skin irritation. Look for this plant along the road between Rising Sun and the village of St. Mary.

FIREWEED
Chamerion angustifolium
Evening-primrose Family (Onagraceae)

Description: Fireweed is a tall perennial herb growing ½–4 feet tall from spreading rhizomes, often forming large colonies. The numerous leaves are arranged alternately on the stem. They are lance-shaped, 2–6 inches long and have entire (toothless) margins. Pink to magenta flowers form terminal spikes (racemes) blooming from the bottom upward. Each flower is 1–1½ inches wide with 4 broad petals, 8 stamens and a 4-lobed stigma. Fruits are linear capsules 1–4 inches long. Seeds are dispersed by wind, aided by a tuft of slender hairs growing from the tip. Fireweed blooms from July through September.

Habitat: Abundant in avalanche chutes, along streams and on open slopes at all elevations below alpine; an early colonizer of freshly burned areas.

Notes: Fireweed produces hundreds of seeds per capsule. When the pods split these seeds are carried for miles by mountain breezes and quickly colonize open, freshly disturbed ground. This plant's common name derives from its ability to flourish in recently burned forests. Herbalists use fireweed leaves in tea to relieve digestive problems and as a wash to heal skin irritation. It is known as *Epilobium angustifolium* by some botanists. Look for this plant on upper slopes along Going-to-the-Sun Highway.

ALPINE FIREWEED
Chamerion latifolium
Evening-primrose Family
(Onagraceae)

Description: Alpine fireweed is a leafy perennial sprouting from a branched rootcrown. It typically grows to a maximum height of 2 feet. The lance-shaped leaves have entire margins and are 1–2½ inches long. They are opposite each other along the lower stem and extend into the inflorescence (flower cluster). Four-petaled, pink to rose-colored flowers are clustered into a spike at the top of this plant. Petals are ½–1¼ inches long and the flowers are disk-shaped. Long capsules (1¼–4 inches) enclose hundreds of tiny seeds. Alpine fireweed blooms in July and August.

Habitat: Common on gravelly, montane streambanks; also occurs on rocky slopes near treeline; has an affinity for limestone substrates.

Notes: Alpine fireweed is one of the first colonizers of newly formed gravel bars, along with yellow mountain avens (*Dryas drummondii*, pg. 145). It differs from common fireweed (*C. angustifolium*, previous page) in its smaller stature, opposite lower leaves and leafy inflorescence. It's also known as broad-leaved willowherb, and by the scientific name *Epilobium latifolium*.

ALPINE WILLOWHERB
Epilobium anagallidifolium
Evening-primrose Family
(Onagraceae)

Description: Alpine willowherb is a low-growing, mat-forming perennial with leafy stems 1–6 inches high. The herbage often has a purplish cast. Leaves are ½–1 inch long and elliptic in outline with entire (toothless) margins. Only a few flowers are produced in each terminal flower cluster. They are light pink with 4 small petals and hang downward before fully opening. Tiny, slender pods about 1 inch long enclose the seeds. Each seed is tipped with a tuft of fine hair.

Habitat: Gravelly, open slopes and along streams in the subalpine and alpine zones.

Notes: The species name *anagallidifolium* comes from the Latin *anagallis* (unpretentious) and *folium* (leaf), referring to the inelaborate leaves of this tiny plant. Several species of willowherb (*Epilobium* species) grow in similar habitats in Glacier National Park. Many of these plants require a technical plant key and hand lens to distinguish one species from another.

FAIRY SLIPPER
Calypso bulbosa
Orchid Family (Orchidaceae)

Description: Fairy slipper is a delicate perennial with solitary, bright pink flowers on erect, leafless stalks 2–8 inches high. A single, basal leaf is produced, 1–2½ inches long and elliptic in outline. Leaves are produced in autumn and survive through the winter, fading the following summer. The flower is composed of 5 slender, lance-shaped petals and sepals that radiate above a white-and-purple-spotted, pouch-shaped lower lip. The pouch is open at the top and tinged with yellow on the inside. In fruit, this plant produces a club-shaped capsule less than ½ inch long. Fairy slipper blooms in May and June.

Habitat: Shady, moist mountain forests from montane to subalpine.

Notes: Fairy slipper lures pollinators (mainly bees) with its sweet-smelling flower, but provides no nectar reward. The highly variable patterning of purple spots is thought to be a means of fooling bees into visiting more than one or two nectarless flowers. The genus name *Calypso* means "concealment" in Greek, referring to the inconspicuous nature of this often overlooked plant. These plants are extremely fragile. Picking or trampling the flowers can easily damage the bulb and kill the plant.

NARROW-LEAVED COLLOMIA
Collomia linearis
Phlox Family (Polemoniaceae)

Description: Narrow-leaved collomia is a small, slender annual with short-hairy herbage, growing 4–16 inches tall. The narrowly lance-shaped leaves are 1–2 inches long and have entire (toothless) margins. They are arranged alternately along the stem and lack petioles. Flowers are usually pink but may be almost white or tinged with purple. They are 5-petaled, funnel-shaped and ¼–½ inch long. Flowers are clustered in a terminal, leafy inflorescence, hemispheric in shape, and typically bloom in June and July.

Habitat: Common in a wide variety of partially sunny habitats in the montane zone such as streambanks, open forests, shrublands and on rock outcrops.

Notes: Narrow-leaved collomia is one of the first annual plants to colonize disturbed ground on sunny, open sites. A similar plant, pink twink (*Microsteris gracilis*), resembles narrow-leaved collomia but has mostly opposite leaves and small flower clusters in the axils of upper leaves. Both species occupy very similar habitats.

ALPINE LEWISIA
Lewisia pygmaea
Purslane Family (Portulacaceae)

Description: Alpine lewisia is a short, taprooted perennial growing ½–1½ inches tall. A pair of narrow, leaf-like bracts grows opposite each other along the stem between the flower and basal leaves. Numerous basal leaves are produced, each up to 3 inches long and linear in outline. Solitary, pink to magenta flowers are produced in July and August. They have 6–8 petals and are less than 1 inch in diameter. Flowers are subtended by 2 sepals that have gland-toothed margins.

Habitat: Open slopes and rock ledges where spring runoff keeps the soil moist; montane to alpine zones.

Notes: The genus name *Lewisia* honors Capt. Meriwether Lewis. Captain Lewis made many important botanical discoveries during his search with William Clark for the elusive Northwest Passage. Another member of the genus *Lewisia* is the Montana state flower, bitterroot (*L. rediviva*). Bitterroot has much larger flowers, prefers well-drained, gravelly sites such as grasslands and is only known to occur in Glacier National Park near Marias Pass. Look for alpine lewisia near Logan Pass on lush, wet, rock outcrops and ledges.

SMALL-LEAVED MINER'S LETTUCE
Montia parvifolia
Purslane Family (Portulacaceae)

Description: Small-leaved miner's lettuce is a delicate perennial with spreading stolons (runners) and ascending to lax stems growing 2–12 inches long. Basal leaves are ½–1 inch long and elliptic in outline. The stem leaves are smaller and lance-shaped, often with small plantlets tucked between stem and leaf petiole. Light pink, 5-petaled flowers are about ½ inch wide and bloom June to August.

Habitat: Moist mountain slopes, stream banks and rock outcrops from montane to near treeline; common in moist, shallow, mossy soil.

Notes: The small plantlets produced in the leaf axils of miner's lettuce drop to the ground and readily establish in mossy soil. Narrow-leaved miner's lettuce (*M. linearis*) is another species that grows in Glacier National Park, in drier habitats. It is a small annual with linear leaves and smaller flowers (less than ¼ inch wide) that are produced in 1-sided clusters.

FEW-FLOWERED SHOOTING STAR
Dodecatheon pulchellum
Primrose Family (Primulaceae)

Description: Few-flowered shooting star is a slender perennial herb with distinctive flowers on stems 2–14 inches tall. Leaves are all basal and narrowly lance-shaped to oblong in outline, growing 1–6 inches long. Few to several flowers are born on stalks of equal length at the tip of naked stems. Each flower bears five pink to magenta petals that are united at the base and reflexed backward exposing a yellow ring and 5 fused, yellow anthers. Seeds are released from the egg-shaped capsule through 5 vertical slits. This plant blooms from June through August.

Habitat: Moist mountain meadows and along streams from montane to alpine.

Notes: Few-flowered shooting star is also called woodland shooting star. Alpine plants are shorter and have fewer flowers. Desert shooting star (*D. conjugens*) grows in drier habitats within Glacier National Park and looks similar to few-flowered shooting star but has glandular-hairy leaves. Its capsules release seeds from a small hole in the top, instead of through 5 slits.

MEADOW RUE
Thalictrum occidentale
Buttercup Family (Ranunculaceae)

Description: Meadow rue is a rhizomatous perennial with leafy, erect stems growing 12–31 inches tall. The leaves are divided 2–4 times into groups of 3 wedge-shaped, lobed leaflets, each ½–1 inch long. Male and female flowers are on separate plants. Both types have 4–5 greenish, inconspicuous sepals, no petals and are produced in loose, branched, terminal clusters (panicles). The female flowers (pictured)have a purplish green group of 4–9 ovaries that swell into a star-shaped cluster of beaked achenes when fertilized. Male flowers have clusters of long, dangling anthers hanging from each flower.

Habitat: Abundant in montane and subalpine forests; common in avalanche chutes and meadows and on open slopes.

Notes: The leaves of meadow rue are easily mistaken for columbine leaves (see pg. 142), which have a similar divided and lobed pattern. Columbines, however, have much showier flowers than the delicate meadow rue. The aroma of this plant appealed to some Native American tribes, who used it as perfume.

PRAIRIE SMOKE
Geum triflorum
Rose Family (Rosaceae)

Description: Prairie smoke is a perennial herb with soft-hairy foliage and pinkish stems growing 6–12 inches tall. Most leaves are basal and 2–8 inches long. They are pinnately divided into many delicate, lobed leaflets, appearing almost lacy. Stem leaves are reduced to one small pair. Three nodding, cup-shaped flowers are produced per stem in May to July. They are about ½ inch long with flesh-colored petals nearly hidden by the pinkish purple calyx and barely open even at full bloom. Fruit are tiny achenes tipped with a feathery beak, 1–1½ inches long.

Habitat: Open grasslands and meadows from montane to subalpine zones.

Notes: Clusters of achenes form feathery plumes (inset), giving prairie smoke its descriptive common name. It's also called old man's whiskers. Native Americans used the roots in an eyewash solution and crushed the seeds for perfume.

WOOD'S ROSE
Rosa woodsii
Rose Family (Rosaceae)

Description: Wood's rose is a prickly, deciduous shrub with stems 1–5 feet high. It is armored with pairs of large, hooked spines just below the leaf nodes and with smaller prickles between nodes. The leaves are pinnately divided into 5–9 toothed leaflets, each ½–1½ inches long and ovate in outline. Many of the teeth along the leaflet margin are tipped with tiny glands. Clusters of 2–5 pink to magenta, 5-petaled flowers are produced at branch tips. Each flower is 1–2 inches wide, blooming in June and July. The fruit of the plant is a round, red, berry-like "rose hip" tipped with persistent sepals.

Habitat: Moist, open sites from montane to lower subalpine; common in forest openings and bordering wetlands, streams and grasslands.

Notes: Wood's rose is quick to colonize open, disturbed ground, especially in moist conditions. Another common rose of Glacier National Park is prickly rose (*R. acicularis*). It has solitary flowers and lacks the stout, hooked spines found on the stems of Wood's rose, bearing instead softer, bristly prickles. Baldhip rose (*R. gymnocarpa*, inset) grows in Glacier's mountain forests. Baldhip rose is easy to recognize in fruit, because its fruit are not tipped with persistent sepals like most other roses. Rose hips are high in vitamins, especially vitamin C, and are often used in tea preparations to ward off colds and flu.

RED MONKEYFLOWER
Mimulus lewisii
Figwort Family (Scrophulariaceae)

Description: Red monkeyflower is a rhizomatous perennial with sticky, long-hairy foliage and stems growing 8–32 inches tall. Its leaves are ovate in outline, 1–2½ inches long and opposite each other along the stem. There are obvious, parallel veins running from the base to the tip of the leaves. Monkeyflower's tubular or vase-shaped flowers are pinkish red with yellow throats. They are 1–2 inches long and strongly 2-lipped. The upper lip has 2 erect lobes, and the lower lip has 3 spreading lobes. Flowers arise from the axils of upper leaves and typically bloom in July and August.

Habitat: Abundant in wet mountain meadows and along streams just below treeline; less common at lower elevations.

Notes: Red monkeyflower is the only red or purplish species of monkeyflower in Glacier National Park. The other five species are yellow. It is one of Glacier's most showy wildflowers, creating brilliant displays of color along subalpine streams and wet meadows. The plant's scientific name honors Capt. Meriwether Lewis of the Lewis and Clark Expedition. Another popular common name is Lewis's monkeyflower. Look for this plant on wet, drippy cliffs along the upper reaches of Going-to-the-Sun Road.

ELEPHANT'S-HEAD
Pedicularis groenlandica
Figwort Family (Scrophulariaceae)

Description: Elephant's-head is an erect, perennial herb with slender stems growing 4–24 inches tall. Its leaves are 1–8 inches long and deeply lobed into lance-shaped, toothed segments. Leaves grow in an alternate pattern along the stem. Dense clusters of magenta flowers are borne at stem tops. Each flower is about ½ inch long and strongly resembles an elephant's head. The upper lip has a distinctive upturned, tubular beak (elephant's trunk) and the lower lip has 2 broad, lateral lobes (elephant's ears). Elephant's-head blooms in July and August.

Habitat: Wet mountain meadows and fens; common at elevations up to the lower alpine zone.

Notes: These plants were given the species name *groenlandica* because they were first discovered in Greenland. The distinctive flower of elephant's-head makes these plants easy to identify when they are flowering.

SHOWY ASTER
Aster conspicuus
Sunflower Family (Asteraceae)

Description: Showy aster is a robust perennial herb growing 11–27 inches tall from thick rhizomes. Stiff hair and tiny, yellowish glands are produced on the upper stem. Many triangular, toothed, rough-feeling leaves grow in an alternate arrangement along the stem. They are elliptic in outline, 3–5 inches long and gradually get smaller toward the top. Flowers are arranged in a head typical of the Sunflower family. The outer ray flowers are purple, while the inner disk flowers are yellow. Green bracts surrounding each flower head are arranged in an overlapping pattern similar to roof shingles. Flower heads are loosely clustered at the tops of stems. Showy aster blooms in July and August.
Habitat: Abundant on both sides of the Continental Divide in dry to moist forests, usually from montane to lower subalpine.
Notes: Showy aster usually doesn't flower in the shade of a forest understory, but the leafy stems grow quite well. Large patches of this plant (without flowers) are very common in the understory of Douglas fir and subalpine fir forests. Abundant flowering occurs following a canopy disturbance such as fire or windthrow, or along trails and roads. This plant provides important winter forage for elk.

LEAFY ASTER
Aster foliaceus
Sunflower Family (Asteraceae)

Description: Leafy aster is a perennial herb with erect stems growing up to 2 feet high. Its foliage may be hairless or slightly hairy. Leaves are broadly lance-shaped in outline, 2–5 inches long and have entire (toothless) margins. Lower leaves are larger and usually have broad petioles (stalks), while the upper leaves clasp the stem and gradually become smaller toward the top. A loose cluster of several flower heads is produced at the top of the plant. Each flower head has yellow disk flowers arranged in a tight, central button. Bluish purple ray flowers surround them and are each ½–¾ inch long. Leaf-like bracts (involucral bracts) surround each flower head in a shingled, overlapping pattern. The outermost row of bracts is longest, with several robust, leafy bracts that may be as long as the innermost row.

Habitat: Abundant in moist mountain meadows and open forest; montane to subalpine zones.

Notes: The outer row of long, leaf-like involucral bracts surrounding the flower heads sets this species apart from most of the other asters in Glacier National Park. Eaton's aster (*A. eatonii*) also has long, leaf-like involucral bracts, but its leaves are linear in outline instead of lance-shaped, and it grows at lower elevations than leafy aster. Eaton's aster is much less common than leafy aster in the park.

ARCTIC ASTER
Aster sibiricus
Sunflower Family (Asteraceae)

Description: Arctic aster is a low-growing perennial with short-hairy herbage. Its leaves are lance-shaped, 1–2 inches long and somewhat stiff. Lower leaves are small with short petioles and wither soon after the plant blooms. Several flower heads are produced in a loose cluster at the top of the stem. Each flower head consists of a central button of yellow disk flowers surrounded by 12–23 purple ray flowers. Leaf-like involucral bracts, tinged with purple, surround each flower head in an overlapping, shingle-like pattern. Arctic aster blooms in August and September.

Habitat: Common in rocky soil of subalpine and alpine meadows, slopes, ridges and streambanks.

Notes: Arctic aster and leafy aster (*A. foliaceus*, previous page) are Glacier's two most common high-elevation aster species. Arctic aster resembles some members of the flea-bane genus (*Erigeron* species) that grow in the same habitat and can easily be confused with these plants. Arctic aster typically blooms later than these fleabane species, and its ray flowers are less numerous.

SPOTTED KNAPWEED
Centaurea maculosa
Sunflower Family (Asteraceae)

Description: Spotted knapweed is a perennial herb with highly branched stems growing 1–3 feet tall from a taproot. Its foliage is sparsely hairy. A basal rosette of grayish, hairy leaves is produced when plants first sprout. In larger, older plants the leaves grow in an alternate arrangement along the stem and branches. All leaves are pinnately divided into small, lance-shaped segments. Many flower heads are produced per plant, each at the tip of a separate branch. Flower heads are about 1 inch wide and are composed of many tightly clustered, purplish pink disk flowers. The outer disk flowers are enlarged and appear somewhat petal-like. Spotted knapweed blooms in July and August.

Habitat: Open, montane woodlands, grasslands and meadows; often grows in disturbed sites adjacent to roads or trails.

Notes: Spotted knapweed is a well-known noxious weed throughout the northwest. If left unchecked, this weed can virtually replace all native species within a few years. Its invasion into Glacier National Park's native communities is still somewhat modest, and park staff vigilantly monitor its progress. The meadows near Rising Sun are checked for spotted knapweed populations regularly, since this plant is especially aggressive in grasslands. The weed is then either pulled by hand or spot-sprayed with herbicide. The spiny bracts on the flower heads contain an allergen that, when directly contacted, causes an irritating reaction in some people.

SUBALPINE FLEABANE
Erigeron peregrinus
Sunflower Family (Asteraceae)

Description: Subalpine fleabane is a perennial that grows from short, fibrous rhizomes. Stems grow up to 27 inches tall and bear solitary, showy, purple and yellow flower heads. The leaves are highly variable, ranging from elongated to spoon-shaped in outline. Basal leaves are largest (up to 8 inches), gradually becoming smaller toward the top of the stem. Flower heads are about 1 inch wide with purple ray flowers along the perimeter and yellow disk flowers clustered in the center of each head. The leaf-like involucral bracts surrounding each flower head are dotted with tiny hair and glands, and feel slightly sticky. Subalpine fleabane blooms in July and August.

Habitat: Abundant in moist soil of lush, subalpine meadows, such as those near Logan Pass Visitor Center.

Notes: Subalpine fleabane is very visible when Glacier's high-elevation meadows bloom. It's often seen in rich displays with paintbrush and arnica in moist meadows and along streams. Subalpine fleabane is sometimes mistaken for leafy aster (*Aster foliaceus*, pg. 181), also common in these habitats. One can differentiate between the two species by examining the involucral bracts surrounding each flower head. The involucral bracts of subalpine fleabane are sticky-feeling due to the presence of tiny glandular hairs. Leafy aster usually has more than one head per stem and does not have glandular involucral bracts.

ALPINE DAISY
Erigeron simplex
Sunflower Family (Asteraceae)

Description: Alpine daisy is a tiny plant with a solitary, showy flower head perched on sticky-hairy stems up to 6 inches tall. Its leaves are up to 2 inches long and narrowly oblong in outline. Most leaves arise from the plant base, but a few may be scattered along the stem. Flower heads are about 1½ inches across and composed of 50–125 lavender ray flowers surrounding a central cluster of bright yellow disk flowers. A row of tiny, densely long-hairy, leaf-like involucral bracts surrounds the base of each flower head. Alpine daisy typically blooms in July.

Habitat: Common in alpine meadows and on slopes near the Continental Divide.

Notes: This small but brilliantly colored plant has a relatively short period of time in which to grow, bloom and set seed. It devotes a tremendous amount of resources to producing large, showy flowers that will attract pollinators before winter returns.

PARRY'S TOWNSENDIA
Townsendia parryi
Sunflower Family (Asteraceae)

Description: Parry's townsendia is a taprooted, low-growing perennial up to 8 inches tall with hairy herbage. The leaves are mostly basal, narrowly spoon-shaped in outline and 1–2½ inches long. The single flower head per stem is usually quite large (up to 2 inches in diameter), with purple ray flowers around the perimeter and yellow disk flowers in the center of each head. The small, leaf-like bracts surrounding each flower head (involucral bracts) bear a distinct fringe of hair along their margins. Parry's townsendia blooms June to August.

Habitat: Common in sparsely vegetated soil of grasslands, meadows and open forest in the montane zone; often on gravel terraces adjacent to streams; less common at higher elevations.

Notes: The flower head of Parry's townsendia is often large relative to the rest of the plant. Townsendia flowers are very similar to those of asters (*Aster* species) and fleabanes (*Erigeron* species). Townsendias typically have larger flower heads (over ½ inch high) and smaller leaves (less than ¼ inch wide) than fleabanes.

STICKSEED
Hackelia micrantha
Borage Family (Boraginaceae)

Description: Stickseed is a robust herbaceous perennial (sometimes biennial) with several stems growing up to 3 feet tall from a branched rootcrown. Its herbage is hairy. Broadly lance-shaped leaves are up to 8 inches long, becoming progressively smaller toward the top of the stem. Numerous delicate flowers, blue with yellow centers, are loosely arranged at the top of the stem. Flowers are about ¼ inch in diameter and composed of 5 spreading petals which come together at the base to form a small tube. Seeds are borne within hard, prickled fruit (nutlets). Stickseed blooms June to August.

Habitat: Moist aspen groves on the eastern side of Glacier National Park; open forests and grasslands in the montane zone.

Notes: The flowers of stickseed resemble those of forget-me-nots (*Myosotis* species, following page). Forget-me-nots lack prickled fruit, instead forming nutlets that are smooth and shiny. The barbed nutlets of stickseed readily adhere to the fur of passing animals (and hikers), aiding in the dispersal of its seeds.

BLUEBELLS
Mertensia oblongifolia
Borage Family (Boraginaceae)

Description: Bluebells produces several ascending stems, growing up to 12 inches tall, from a branched root. Its bluish green leaves are lance-shaped in outline and up to 6 inches long at the plant base. Stem leaves gradually get smaller toward the top. Basal leaves are stalked (with a petiole), while stem leaves are directly attached at the blade base. Purplish-blue flowers hang in branched clusters from the top of the flowering stem. Each flower is ½–¾ inch long and funnel-shaped with flaring lobes toward the tip. Bluebells blooms in June and July.

Habitat: Mid- to upper-elevation grasslands, meadows and open forest; more common east of the Continental Divide.

Notes: The leaves of bluebells are considered edible, but may be toxic in large quantities. This species is also referred to as "lungwort." Early herbalists believed that, since the leaves vaguely resemble lungs, this plant could cure respiratory ailments.

✕ MOUNTAIN FORGET-ME-NOT
Myosotis alpestris
Borage Family (Boraginaceae)

Description: Mountain forget-me-not produces tufts of stems that grow 2–8 inches tall. Its foliage is covered with short hair. Leaves are lance- to spoon-shaped in outline, stalked, and up to 2 inches long. Most of them form a basal rosette. A few stem leaves are smaller, stalkless and grow in an alternate arrangement. Flowers are blue with a yellow (sometimes white) center and arranged in a branched, 1-sided display that uncoils with age. Each flower is less than ¼ inch wide with five flaring lobes fused at the base into a short tube. Mountain forget-me-not blooms June to August.

Habitat: Common in meadows and on rocky slopes at high-elevation.

Notes: Mountain forget-me-not is the state flower of Alaska. The flower color and structure of this species and many others in the borage family help facilitate pollination by guiding insects toward the flower tube. As insects search for nectar within the tube they pick up pollen. This pollen is deposited on the stigma of the next flower the insect visits. The garden forget-me-not is a close relative of this montane native.

LYALL'S ROCKCRESS
Arabis lyallii
Mustard Family (Brassicaceae)

Description: Lyall's rockcress is a tufted perennial with stems growing up to 8 inches high from a branched rootcrown. The numerous basal leaves are smooth and hairless, oblong in outline, slightly fleshy, and up to 1¼ inches long. Stem leaves clasp the stem at the base. Only a few purple, 4-petaled flowers are produced on each stem. Each flower is ¼–½ inch long. Slender, erect pods 1–2½ inches long are produced in late summer. Lyall's rockcress blooms June to August.

Habitat: Common near or above treeline in rocky, sparsely vegetated soil.

Notes: Two other rockcress species grow in similar habitats: reflexed rockcress (*A. holboellii*, pg. 62) and Lemmon's rockcress (*A. lemmonii*). Reflexed rockcress has fruit (pods) that hang downward when mature. Its flowers are white to pinkish, and its leaves are narrowly lance-shaped in outline. The pods of Lemmon's rockcress may extend horizontally or hang slightly downward. It is a small species (less than 8 inches tall), with broadly spoon-shaped leaves covered with branching hair.

HAREBELL
Campanula rotundifolia
Bellflower Family (Campanulaceae)

Description: Harebell is a slender, delicate perennial with milky sap. Stems are typically 8–12 inches tall, but can grow to 20 inches. Harebell's basal leaves are narrowly spoon-shaped in outline, up to ¾ inch long and wither soon after the plant flowers. The more conspicuous stem leaves are much narrower and up to 2 inches long. A few nodding blue flowers are produced on stalks toward the top of the stem. Each flower has five petals united into a bell shape ½–1 inch long. Harebell blooms in July and August.
Habitat: Open forests, grasslands, exposed ridges and slopes at all elevations.
Notes: Small tufts of harebell leaves, without a flower for reference, often look like tufts of grass. Pluck a single leaf tip and milky sap will ooze from this plant, indicating its true identity. This characteristic, along with the large, bell-shaped flowers and linear stem leaves, are the most distinguishing features of harebell. The generic name *Campanula* comes from the Latin word *campana,* "a bell," referring to the flower shape. The specific name *rotundifolia* means "round leaves" describing the basal leaves. Native Americans used the leaves to treat coughs and tuberculosis.

BOURGEAU'S MILK-VETCH
Astragalus bourgovii
Pea Family (Fabaceae)

Description: Bourgeau's milk-vetch is a perennial herb with finely hairy foliage and stems up to 12 inches high. Its leaves are arranged in an alternate pattern along the stem and divided into 13–23 lance-shaped leaflets. Each leaflet is ½–¾ inch long. Five to ten purple and white flowers are produced above the leaves in an elongated, lax inflorescence. Each flower is about ½ inch long and composed of a large upper banner petal, 2 lateral wing petals and 2 lower keel petals that are fused along the lower edge. Flattened, elliptic pods are produced in late summer. Pods are approximately ½ inch long and covered with black hair. Bourgeau's milk-vetch blooms June to August.

Habitat: Rocky, often moist soil of meadows, ridges and open slopes near or above treeline; occasionally occurs at lower elevations on the east side of the Continental Divide.

Notes: There are 12 different species of milk-vetch (*Astragalus* species) in Glacier National Park, most of which require a hand lens and technical plant key to differentiate. Bourgeau's milk-vetch is one of the most common high-elevation species of milk-vetch in the park.

SILKY LUPINE
Lupinus sericeus
Pea Family (Fabaceae)

Description: Silky lupine is a perennial herb growing 8–24 inches tall with silky-hairy herbage. Its leaves are divided into 5–10 narrow leaflets, all originating from one point like fingers on the palm of a hand (palmate leaf arrangement). Leaflets are covered with long, flat-lying hair on both the upper and lower surfaces. Purple flowers are produced in whorls along an erect flowering stalk. Each flower is about ½ inch long and has a typical Pea family flower structure with a large upper banner petal, 2 lateral wing petals and 2 lower keel petals that are fused along the lower edge. The banner petal is distinctly upturned and hairy on its back surface. Silky pods about 1 inch long are produced in late summer and contain 3–6 seeds each. Silky lupine blooms in June and July.
Habitat: Common throughout Glacier National Park in meadows, grasslands and open forests of the montane zone.
Notes: A related species, silvery lupine (*L. argenteus*), is very similar in appearance to silky lupine. Silvery lupine is typically larger and its banner petal is hairless and less strongly upturned. Wild lupines have been known to cause fatalities in domestic livestock and can be poisonous to humans if taken internally. Young children are particularly susceptible because lupine seed pods resemble those of garden peas. The young leaves, seeds and pods are especially toxic.

SHOWY LOCOWEED
Oxytropis splendens
Pea Family (Fabaceae)

Description: Showy locoweed is an herbaceous perennial that grows 4–12 inches high and is densely clothed in long, erect hairs. Its leaves are primarily basal and 2–10 inches long. Each leaf has numerous whorls of 3–5 leaflets. Leaflets are about ½ inch long. Narrow, elongated clusters (racemes) of 12–35 magenta flowers are produced along leafless flowering stems. Each flower is roughly ½ inch long and has a typical Pea family flower structure, with an upper banner petal, two lateral wing petals and two lower petals that are fused along the lower side. Seed pods are egg-shaped in outline, erect and ½–¾ inch long. Showy locoweed typically blooms in July.

Habitat: Common in grasslands and on gravelly streambanks in the montane zone.

Notes: Its whorled, silky-hairy leaflets distinguish showy locoweed from the other 5 locoweeds found in Glacier National Park. All locoweeds are poisonous to livestock and have resulted in mortality of horses, sheep and cattle. Nor should humans ingest these plants.

AMERICAN VETCH
Vicia americana
Pea Family (Fabaceae)

Description: American vetch is a climbing or trailing perennial with slender stems. Its leaves are arranged alternately and are pinnately divided into 8–14 narrow leaflets. Each leaflet is ½–1¼ inches long. The leaves are terminated by 1–3 curling, gripping tendrils which enable the plant to spread and climb. Clusters of purple flowers grow from leaf axils. Each flower is ½–1 inch long and is shaped like a typical Pea family flower, with an upper banner petal, 2 lateral wing petals and 2 lower petals that are fused along the lower edge. The flowers of this plant have a strongly upturned banner petal. Flattened pods 1–1½ inches long are produced in late summer and fall. American vetch blooms in June and July.

Habitat: Common in montane meadows, grasslands, shrublands and open forests.

Notes: The genus name *Vicia* comes from the Latin word *vincio,* "to bind," referring to the way this plant uses binding tendrils to scale objects and other plants. While not generally considered poisonous, this plant contains compounds that are toxic in large quantities and should be viewed with caution.

EXPLORER'S GENTIAN

Gentiana calycosa
Gentian Family (Gentianaceae)

Description: Explorer's gentian is a slender, perennial herb with clustered, erect stems growing 4–12 inches high. Leaves are egg- or heart-shaped in outline, ½–1 inch long and arranged opposite each other along the stem. The lowest leaves are sometimes joined together at the base, gripping the stem. A single, erect, deep blue flower is borne on the tip of each stem. Flowers are 1–2 inches long and funnel-shaped with fringed clefts between 5 lobes that line the perimeter. Explorer's gentian blooms in July and August.

Habitat: Moist, open sites at high elevation, such as wet, alpine meadows and along streams; open subalpine forest where snow lies late.

Notes: Gentian has been used medicinally for centuries to stimulate digestion. It was also thought to remedy "female weakness and hysteria." Overdoses may cause nausea and vomiting.

NORTHERN GENTIAN

Gentianella amarella
Gentian Family (Gentianaceae)

Description: Northern gentian is a delicate, slender, annual herb with ascending stems growing up to 16 inches high. Lance-shaped leaves ½–1½ inches long occur opposite each other along the stem. The lavender flowers arise singly from axils of upper leaves. They are tubular, ½–¾ inch long and have a fine fringe of hair inside the corolla tube. Northern gentian blooms June to August.

Habitat: Meadows, grasslands, shrublands and open forests at all elevations.

Notes: Another *Gentianella* species, four-parted gentian (*G. propinqua*), is similar in appearance to northern gentian, but does not have a fringe of hair in the corolla tube. Northern gentian was formerly placed within the *Gentiana* genus and has many medicinal uses common to those plants. For hundreds of years, these plants were used to treat digestive ailments, fever and skin diseases. Many modern herbalists still use gentians to relieve these conditions.

BALLHEAD WATERLEAF
Hydrophyllum capitatum
Waterleaf Family
(Hydrophyllaceae)

Description: Ballhead waterleaf is a low-growing perennial with hairy herbage and stems 4–10 inches high. The leaves are 2–8 inches long and pinnately divided into lobed leaflets. Globe-shaped clusters of bluish purple flowers grow from below the leaves. Each flower is cup-shaped and about ½ inch long with stamens projecting well past the petals. Ballhead waterleaf blooms May to July.

Habitat: Common in moist soil of forests, shrublands and grasslands; often occurs where soil has been disturbed, as along trails or in soil slumps; montane to subalpine.

Notes: The spherical flowerheads of ballhead waterleaf appear fuzzy due to the long stamens projecting from each flower. Native Americans and early settlers used the roots, young leaves and shoots of ballhead waterleaf for food.

SILKY PHACELIA
Phacelia sericea
Waterleaf Family
(Hydrophyllaceae)

Description: Silky phacelia is a slender, erect perennial growing up to 16 inches high. Its herbage is covered with long, silky hair. Leaves are less than 6 inches long and pinnately divided into linear segments. Most leaves occur in a dense basal rosette, with stem leaves gradually smaller toward the top of the stem. An elongated cluster (raceme) of purple flowers occurs at the top of flowering stems. Bowl-shaped flowers are about ¼ inch long and bear yellow-tipped stamens that project well past the petals. Silky phacelia blooms in July and August.

Habitat: Dry, rocky, open slopes; talus and gravelly streambanks; montane to alpine.

Notes: Another phacelia common in Glacier National Park, silver-leaved phacelia (*P. hastata*), is very similar to silky phacelia but has narrowly lance-shaped leaves with entire margins (without lobes). Silver-leaved phacelia also grows in rocky, shallow soil of open sites and is found at all elevations.

BLUE-EYED GRASS
Sisyrinchium montanum
Iris Family (Iridaceae)

Description: Blue-eyed grass is a perennial with tufts of erect, stiff, flattened stems growing 4–20 inches tall. The leaves are folded lengthwise and arise from the plant base. They are less than ¼ inch wide, linear and grass-like. Blue, 6-petaled flowers about ½ inch wide are produced singly or in groups of 2–5 near the top of the stem. Each flower has a short stalk and a yellow center. Two leaf-like bracts of unequal size subtend the flowers. Round capsules are formed in fruit, each less than ¼ inch wide. Blue-eyed grass blooms in June and July.

Habitat: Moist mountain grasslands and meadows.

Notes: The delicate blooms of blue-eyed grass are a delight to see in moist mountain meadows. Native Americans used this plant to relieve digestive disorders; modern herbalists use it to treat menstrual problems.

FIELD MINT
Mentha arvensis
Mint Family (Lamiaceae)

Description: Field mint is a rhizomatous perennial with hairy-glandular herbage and a square stem. It is very aromatic and grows up to 2 feet tall. Lance-shaped, toothed leaves are ¾–2½ inches long and arranged opposite each other along the stem. Purplish pink to blue flowers occur in clusters from leaf axils and are cup-shaped with 4 petal-like lobes. Elongated stamens project well past the petals. Field mint blooms July to September.

Habitat: Common in wet soil along streams, fens and in wet meadows in the montane zone.

Notes: This plant is the source of the minty aroma one sometimes smells when walking along moist seeps or stream banks. Native Americans used field mint tea to treat a variety of discomforts, including nausea, dizziness and colds. They applied it topically to relieve pain and swelling. Some herbalists use field mint to flavor meat, tea and jelly.

WILD BERGAMOT
Monarda fistulosa
Mint Family (Lamiaceae)

Description: Wild bergamot is a slender perennial producing shrubby clusters of square stems 12–28 inches tall. The leaves are lance-shaped in outline, toothed, and occur opposite one another on the stem. The lavender to pinkish purple flowers are produced in a hemispheric cluster 1–3 inches in diameter. Each flower is tubular with two lips. This plant has a distinct, minty aroma, blooming in July and August.

Habitat: Common in montane grasslands and open forest.

Notes: Native Americans had many medicinal uses for wild bergamot, using it to treat colic, fevers, colds, insomnia, heart trouble and nosebleeds. The Blackfeet Indians used a poultice of the leaves for acne. This plant also makes a beautiful addition to native gardens and is easy to propagate from seed. Wild bergamot is also known as bee balm and horse mint.

SELF-HEAL
Prunella vulgaris
Mint Family (Lamiaceae)

Description: Self-heal is a perennial herb growing 4–12 inches tall from branched rootcrowns or short rhizomes. The herbage is sparsely hairy and the main stem is 4-sided. Lance-shaped leaves are 1–3 inches long and occur opposite each other along the stem. They gradually become narrower upward. Purple flowers are clustered in a terminal spike, subtended by leaf-like, often purplish bracts. Each flower is about ½ inch long and tubular with a large, hood-like upper lip and a 3-lobed lower lip. Self-heal blooms June to August.

Habitat: Moist forests, meadows and streambanks in the montane zone.

Notes: This plant's two popular common names, self-heal and heal-all, come from its wide array of medicinal qualities. It has been used to alleviate such conditions as nausea, diarrhea, fever and sore throats. Applied topically, it speeds healing of bruises, rashes and skin ulcers.

BUTTERWORT
Pinguicula vulgaris
Bladderwort Family
(Lentibulariaceae)

Description: Butterwort leaves form a small basal rosette. Its sticky, yellowish leaves are oblong in outline, 1–2 inches long and have inrolled margins. The upper surface is covered with a greasy slime. Purple, funnel-shaped flowers are solitary on leafless stems and bloom in July and August. They are slightly 2-lipped and resemble violet flowers.

Habitat: Moist to wet soil of cliff ledges and streambanks; wet meadows and fens; subalpine and alpine zones; less common lower.

Notes: Butterworts supplement their photosynthetic diet with nutrients obtained through the digestion of small insects. Sticky glands on the leaf surface trap tiny victims. Their struggles stimulate the release of digestive compounds that dissolve tissues into an absorbable liquid.

WILD CHIVES
Allium schoenoprasum
Lily Family (Liliaceae)

Description: Wild chives is a slender perennial herb growing 8–24 inches tall from small, narrowly oval bulbs or clusters of bulbs. Foliage and bulbs have a distinct onion scent. The leaves are less than ¼ inch wide, tubular and hollow. They arise from the plant base and are long and linear, but shorter than the flowering stem. Lavender-colored flowers are clustered in a dense head 1–2 inches wide at the stem tip. Each flower is composed of 6 petal-like, lance-shaped tepals, each just under ½ inch long. In fruit, an oval capsule forms, rounded at the top. Wild chives blooms in July and August.

Habitat: Wet meadows, especially along streams and lakes; abundant in the subalpine zone and common at lower elevations.

Notes: Wild chives closely resembles commercial chives. Many herbalists have collected and added it to food as a flavoring. Both herbalists and Native Americans have used it medicinally. The plant is believed to have antiseptic properties, making it useful as a wound dressing. It also is used to stimulate appetite and aid digestion. A syrup has been made from the plant juices and used to treat coughs and colds. Wild chives are sometimes confused with mountain death camas (*Zigadenus elegans*), which is extremely poisonous.

BLUE CAMAS
Camassia quamash
Lily Family (Liliaceae)

Description: Blue camas is a perennial herb with slender stems 1–2 feet tall sprouting from egg-shaped bulbs. Its leaves arise from the plant base. They are about ½ inch wide, linear and grass-like. Deep blue, star-shaped flowers are arranged in an elongated cluster at the stem top. They have 6 petal-like tepals, each ½–¾ inch long with 3–9 lines (nerves) running from base to tip. As the plant matures the inflorescence elongates. In fruit, egg-shaped capsules develop, each about ½ inch long. Blue camas blooms in June and July.

Habitat: Well-developed soil of moist mountain meadows and grasslands.

Notes: Blue camas was an important food for Native Americans, who cooked and dried the bulbs for use during the winter. They have a sweet flavor reported to be at its peak just after the flowers dry and fall off. Tribal women gathered the bulbs; a young woman's worth as a bride was often elevated by her ability to harvest a large quantity. Early settlers also used blue camas, although not as extensively. Deer and elk graze on the new shoots in early spring. A white-flowered relative, death camas (*Zigadenus elegans*, pg. 83), sometimes grows with blue camas and is extremely poisonous. Look for blue camas in wet meadows near Marias Pass.

WILD BLUE FLAX
Linum lewisii
Flax Family (Linaceae)

Description: Wild blue flax is a slender perennial with delicate, arching stems growing 8–24 inches high. The foliage is grayish green, and plants are usually branched at the base from a woody rootcrown. Tiny, linear, needle-like leaves are arranged alternately along the stem. Pale blue, 5-petaled flowers are produced at the top of stems. The petals are about ½ inch long and fall soon after opening. Seeds are borne in terminal, round capsules. Wild blue flax typically blooms June to August.

Habitat: Open to partially shaded sites at all elevations; common in grasslands and on alpine slopes.

Notes: Wild blue flax produces flowers throughout most of the summer and early fall and has been incorporated into many native gardens. The seeds are rich in oils (alpha-linoleic and cis-linoleic fatty acids) known to have many health benefits. Its European relative, common flax (*L. usitatissimum*), is cultivated for the commercial production of these oils. A few common flax plants were reported in the park in the 1920s, near East Glacier. Native Americans used wild blue flax seeds for food. They also made ropes, mats and other household items from its strong fibers.

SPOTTED CORAL-ROOT
Corallorhiza maculata
Orchid Family (Orchidaceae)

Description: Spotted coral-root is a slender perennial with erect, purplish brown stems 8–24 inches tall sprouting from thick rhizomes that resemble ocean coral. These plants lack chlorophyll so the foliage is not green. Leaves are reduced to small scales. Each plant has 10–30 flowers scattered along the upper portion of the stem. Flowers are composed of 3 erect, petal-like tepals, 2 spreading, wing-like tepals and a lower, white, purple-spotted lip. The lower lip has wavy edges and 2 small basal lobes. Fruits are plump capsules just under ¾ inch long that hang downward on all sides of the stem. Spotted coral-root blooms in June and July.

Habitat: Common in mountain forests in the montane zone; more common on the west side of Glacier National Park.

Notes: Instead of obtaining energy and nutrition through photosynthesis, coral-root plants parasitize soil fungi. Soil fungi invade the plant's roots and extend root-like hyphae out into the forest soil. These hyphae digest dead organic material and are in turn digested by the coral-root plant. A yellow-flowered form of spotted coral-root is common just south of the park.

STRIPED CORAL-ROOT
Corallorhiza striata
Orchid Family (Orchidaceae)

Description: Striped coral-root is an erect, stout perennial with purplish stems 6–16 inches tall. Like other species of coral-root, it doesn't have green foliage. Its leaves are small and scale-like, scattered along the stem. Flowers are loosely clustered along the top portion of the stem. Each flower has 6 pinkish, petal-like tepals with 3–4 dark purple stripes running from base to tip. The lowest tepal is broad and has a rounded spur at the base. In fruit, this plant produces hanging, oval capsules ½–1 inch long. Striped coral-root typically blooms in June.

Habitat: Common in montane forests; more common on the west side of Glacier National Park.

Notes: Striped coral-root obtains energy and nutrients through a parasitic relationship with soil fungi (see notes on spotted coral-root, previous page). All coral-roots depend on this relationship to survive and only grow in forests where organic matter is plentiful. Recent research has shown that spotted coral-root is more common in old-growth forests, while striped coral-root is more prevalent in younger forests.

GIANT HELLEBORINE
Epipactis gigantea
Orchid Family (Orchidaceae)

Description: Giant helleborine is a robust perennial with hairy foliage and stems 12–32 inches tall sprouting from rhizomes. The leaves are lance-shaped in outline, 2–6 inches long and clasp the stem at the leaf base. A loose, linear array (raceme) of 3–15 flowers is produced at the top of the stem. The inflorescence arches at first but straightens as the flowers mature. All flowers are produced on one side of the stem. Each flower is composed of 3 reddish green, lance-shaped sepals, 2 purple, upper petals that are similar to the sepals and a pink, lower, heart-shaped lip petal with 3 prominent lobes. Giant helleborine typically blooms in July.

Habitat: Rare in wet soil of spring-fed fens.

Notes: Giant helleborine is also known as chatterbox due to the jaw-like motion of its hinged lower petal. This plant is rare, known from only one location in Glacier National Park. It has very limited distribution throughout the state and is closely monitored to prevent its extinction in Montana. In Montana and adjacent British Columbia, giant helleborine occurs only around springs that don't freeze in winter. It was first found near Lake McDonald over 100 years ago, but wasn't relocated until 1993.

ONE-FLOWERED BROOMRAPE
Orobanche uniflora
Broomrape Family (Orobanchaceae)

Description: One-flowered broomrape is an annual without chlorophyll. Much of the plant is below ground; only the flower and pedicel (flower stalk) appear above ground. Since this plant lacks chlorophyll, it must obtain its food from other plants capable of photosynthesis. It parasitizes the roots of these plants, withdrawing the food and water it needs for survival and reproduction. One-flowered broomrape has solitary, purple flowers with yellow and white markings. It is 2–8 inches tall and blooms in June and July.

Habitat: Open, moist, often rocky sites on mountain slopes and in the subalpine zone; fairly uncommon and hard to spot due to its limited flowering period; has been observed east of the Continental Divide along the Waterton Lake Trail and west of the divide along the North Fork of the Flathead River.

Notes: Research indicates one-flowered broomrape prefers parasitic hosts in the Saxifrage, Sunflower, Stonecrop and Buttercup families.This plant is also called naked broomrape.

SHOWY JACOB'S LADDER
Polemonium pulcherrimum
Phlox Family (Polemoniaceae)

Description: Showy Jacob's ladder is a perennial herb with tufted stems growing 2–12 inches tall. The leaves are mostly basal and divided into 11–23 oblong leaflets. Each leaflet is about ½ inch long and has entire (toothless) margins. Showy, blue flowers are borne in a hemispheric cluster at the ends of branches. They are funnel-shaped and about ½ inch long and wide with a yellow tube and 5 flaring, purple lobes. Showy Jacob's ladder flowers May to July.

Habitat: Common on dry, open mountain slopes and rock outcrops; less common above treeline on exposed ridges and slopes.

Notes: The foliage of Showy Jacob's ladder has a musky, skunk-like odor, stronger in some populations of the plant than others. The central yellow disk of anthers is useful for guiding insects to that part of the flower, where they receive a dose of pollen along with nectar. Sticky Jacob's ladder (also called sky pilot, *P. viscosum*, inset) has flowers more than ½ inch long and deeply divided leaflets that appear whorled around the main leaf axis. It usually grows at higher elevations than showy Jacob's ladder and is common near or east of the Continental Divide on talus and rocky slopes.

PASQUEFLOWER
Anemone patens
Buttercup Family (Ranunculaceae)

Description: Pasqueflower is a tufted, herbaceous perennial growing 2–10 inches tall with silky-hairy herbage. Its height increases with maturity. Leaf blades are 1–3 inches wide and pinnately divided twice into linear segments, appearing feathery. They are mainly basal, but sometimes occur in a mid-stem whorl. Bluish purple flowers (sometimes white on the inner surface) are solitary on stems, with 5–7 petal-like sepals, each ¾–1½ inches long. They bloom in May and June. In fruit, long, feathery styles remain attached to the achenes, giving the seed heads a fluffy appearance.

Habitat: Montane grasslands; occasionally higher, in subalpine meadows; primarily east of the Continental Divide.

Notes: Pasqueflower is one of the first wildflowers to bloom on foothill prairies along the eastern edge of Glacier National Park. Its blossoms hug the ground, then elongate in fruit to form stalked fuzzy heads later in the summer. This plant is considered poisonous and should not be ingested. Pasqueflower is the state flower of South Dakota. Western pasqueflower (*A. occidentalis*, pg. 94) also occurs in Glacier National Park at higher elevations. It has white flowers instead of bluish purple ones like pasqueflower, and its stem leaves are stalked and more finely divided.

JONES' BLUE COLUMBINE
Aquilegia jonesii
Buttercup Family
(Ranunculaceae)

Description: Jones' blue columbine is a tiny, tufted perennial with glandular, short-hairy herbage, growing to a maximum of 4 inches tall. The leaves are all basal, ¼–½ inch wide and twice divided into crowded, oblong segments. The foliage has a slight blue tinge. Solitary flowers are produced at the top of flowering stems. Each flower has 5 deep blue, spreading sepals and 5 lighter blue, tubular petals. The fruit is a cluster of 5 pod-like capsules, each about ¾ inch long. This plant blooms in June and July.

Habitat: Stony ridges and slopes in the subalpine and alpine zones; prefers calcareous substrates; primarily east of the Continental Divide.

Notes: The tiny, blue-green leaves and large, purplish blue flowers of Jones' blue columbine make this beautiful species very distinctive. It often grows in cushion plant communities on high-elevation, rocky terrain. All parts of columbines, especially the roots and seeds, are considered poisonous.

BLUE CLEMATIS
Clematis occidentalis
Buttercup Family (Ranunculaceae)

Description: Blue clematis is a trailing vine that often climbs shrubs and small trees. Its stems can grow up to 6½ feet long and are somewhat woody. The leaves are divided into 3 lance-shaped leaflets, each 1–3 inches long with faintly toothed margins. The flowers arise singly on long stalks from the base of the upper leaves. Each has 4 purplish blue, petal-like sepals 1–2 inches long. In fruit, small achenes are produced in a dense head, with feathery, persistent styles forming a fluffy plume that may be intact into early winter. Blue clematis blooms May to July.

Habitat: Open forests, shrublands and avalanche chutes; montane to lower subalpine.

Notes: Contact with blue clematis produces irritation in some people with sensitive skin and has been known to cause internal bleeding and even death if taken internally. It is used as an ornamental in northwest native gardens. This plant is also known as blue virgin's bower.

LOW LARKSPUR
Delphinium bicolor
Buttercup Family (Ranunculaceae)

Description: Low larkspur is a slender, erect perennial with stems 4–16 inches high. The leaves are primarily basal and palmately divided into narrowly oblong segments. Leaf blades are 1–2½ inches long with smaller stem leaves. The flowers are arranged in a loose, terminal spike (raceme). Each flower is about 1½ inches across, 1 inch long and composed of 5 large, blue, spreading sepals and 4 petals (the upper 2 white). Seeds are borne within a cluster of finely hairy pods, each about ¾ inch long. Low larkspur typically flowers May to July.

Habitat: Dry grasslands and open slopes from montane to alpine; primarily occurs east of the Continental Divide.

Notes: The four species of larkspur that occur in Glacier National Park are similar and somewhat difficult to differentiate. Low larkspur and Nelson's larkspur (*D. nuttallianum*) are by far the most common. Nelson's larkspur does not have white upper petals (all are blue) and has deeply lobed lower petals. All larkspurs are well known for their toxicity, both for humans and livestock. However, low larkspur blooms early enough and is small enough that it is rarely responsible for poisoning livestock.

BLUE-EYED MARY
Collinsia parviflora
Figwort Family (Scrophulariaceae)

Description: Blue-eyed Mary is an annual herb with slender stems 2–12 inches tall. Stems are often branched and sparsely hairy. The leaf blades are ½–1¼ inches long, broadly linear-shaped and arranged opposite each other along the stem. Upper leaves are sometimes whorled in groups of 3–5. Flowers are 2-lipped and less than ¼ inch long. The upper lip is white, 2-lobed and usually tinged with blue toward the tip. The lower lip is composed of 2 outer lobes and a folded central lobe, all of them blue-violet. Pairs of stalked flowers arise from leaf nodes, and 1–6 flowers may occur in a terminal whorl. Blue-eyed Mary blooms in May and June.

Habitat: Common in moist to dry, sparsely vegetated soil of mountain meadows, forest openings and gravel bars and on rock outcrops.

Notes: Blue-eyed Mary is small and easily overlooked, but its lovely flowers are worth close examination. It has the ability to germinate, grow, flower and set seed in a short period of time (usually within a month), a remarkable advantage in Glacier National Park's short growing season.

ELLIPTIC-LEAVED PENSTEMON
Penstemon ellipticus
Figwort Family (Scrophulariaceae)

Description: Elliptic-leaved penstemon forms mats of prostrate, woody stems and erect, non-woody stems that grow 2–6 inches tall. Its leaves are elliptic in outline and ½–1 inch long. They are smooth and hairless, and sometimes shallowly toothed along the margin. Pairs of stalked, lavender flowers are produced at the tops of stems. The inflorescence is hairy and slightly glandular. Flowers are about 1½ inches long and strongly 2-lipped, with a 2-lobed upper lip and a 3-lobed lower lip. Elliptic-leaved penstemon blooms in July and August.

Habitat: Abundant in stony soil of exposed slopes and moraine and on rock outcrops in the upper subalpine; common in dry, rocky soil at lower elevations.

Notes: The long, tubular flowers of penstemons are pollinated by bees and hummingbirds. The common and generic name *Penstemon* comes from the Latin *penta*, "five" and *stemon*, "stamens," referring to the 5 stamens found within the throat of each flower. Penstemon is the largest genus of vascular plants found only in North America.

ALBERTA PENSTEMON
Penstemon albertinus
Figwort Family (Scrophulariaceae)

Description: Alberta penstemon is a slender perennial with clusters of stems 4–16 inches high. Its basal leaves are ½–1½ inches long, broadly lance-shaped in outline and often have toothed margins. Stem leaves are narrowly lance-shaped and have obscurely toothed margins. Both basal and stem leaves are smooth and somewhat firm. Blue flowers are whorled around the stem in the upper leaf axils. They are long-stalked, about ½ inch long and strongly 2-lipped. The upper lip is 2-lobed and the lower lip is 3-lobed with a pale-colored base. Alberta penstemon blooms in June and July.

Habitat: Common in dry, open forests and grasslands and on rock outcrops in the montane zone; less common at higher elevations.

Notes: Slender blue penstemon (*P. procerus*) occurs in somewhat moister habitats and has a more densely flowered inflorescence than Alberta penstemon. The leaves of slender blue penstemen are narrower than those of Alberta penstemon and have entire margins. Penstemons make beautiful additions to native rock gardens and grow easily from seed.

LYALL'S PENSTEMON
Penstemon lyallii
Figwort Family (Scrophulariaceae)

Description: Lyall's penstemon is a tall, slender perennial growing 12–28 inches high. Stalkless leaves grow in an opposite pattern along the stem. Leaves are narrowly lance-shaped in outline, 1–5 inches long and have toothed margins. The flowers are pale purple to light blue and about 1½ inch long with distinctly wooly anthers. Each flower has a 2-lobed upper lip and a 3-lobed lower lip. Flowers are borne in elongated, one-sided clusters at the tops of stems. Lyall's penstemon typically flowers in July and August.

Habitat: Rocky slopes and outcrops from the montane zone to subalpine.

Notes: The tall, leafy stems, lavender, tubular flowers, and lack of basal leaves distinguish Lyall's penstemon from the other seven species of penstemon found in Glacier National Park. This plant is abundant on rock outcrops and scree slopes along the upper reaches of Going-to-the-Sun Road.

AMERICAN BROOKLIME

Veronica americana
Figwort Family (Scrophulariaceae)

Description: American brooklime is a slender perennial with trailing stems that root at the nodes. Its foliage is smooth and hairless. Leaves are broadly lance-shaped in outline and have toothed margins. They are ½–2½ inches long and have short petioles. Open clusters of flowers (racemes) grow from the axils of upper leaves. Flowers range in color from blue to violet to nearly white and are broadly dish-shaped with 4 spreading lobes. The 2 lower lobes are usually smaller. Each flower is about ¼ inch in diameter. Fruits are smooth, flattened capsules, oval in outline.

Habitat: Common in moist to wet soil along streams, fens and wet meadows; sometimes floating on shallow, slow-moving water.

Notes: The genus name *Veronica* honors St. Veronica. The leaves have a bitter flavor; in Europe and Japan this plant is used often as an addition to salads.

ALPINE VERONICA

Veronica wormskjoldii
Figwort Family (Scrophulariaceae)

Description: Alpine Veronica is a slender, rhizomatous perennial with erect stems 2–10 inches tall and long-hairy herbage. Its leaves are narrowly oval, ½–1¼ inches long and arranged opposite each other along the stem. There are obscure teeth along the margins. Flowers are deep blue and about ½ inch wide with 4 spreading lobes. They are arranged in a short, terminal spike that is slightly sticky to the touch. Fruit are flattened, heart-shaped capsules covered with glandular hair. Alpine Veronica blooms in July and August.

Habitat: Moist meadows and turf near or above treeline; often found near high-elevation streams.

Notes: Another common name for plants of the genus *Veronica* is speedwell, referring to their medicinal qualities. Speedwell has been used for over a century to treat cold and flu symptoms and is very high in Vitamin C.

EARLY BLUE VIOLET
Viola adunca
Violet Family (Violaceae)

Description: Early blue violet is a small, herbaceous perennial spreading by rhizomes, often with lax, leafy stems ½–2 inches long. Its leaves are oval to lance-shaped in outline, have shallowly toothed margins and are ¼–1¼ inches wide. Deep blue to purple flowers arise singly from leaf axils. They are ½–¾ inch wide with 3 spreading lower petals and 2 erect upper petals. There is a sac-like spur at the base of the lowest petal. The style has a distinctive hairy tip. Early blue violet blooms from April to August.

Habitat: Moist mountain meadows, forest openings or open shrublands.

Notes: Early blue violet is one of the first spring flowers to appear in Glacier National Park. Look for it in sunny sites on southern exposures where snow has just receded. Northern bog violet (*V. nephrophylla*) is another common blue-flowered violet in the park. Its flowers are bigger than early blue violet (about 1 inch wide), it lacks leafy stems and is restricted to habitats with permanently wet, peaty soils. Another common violet is Canada violet (*V. canadensis*). It is much larger than early blue violet, has broadly heart-shaped leaves and white flowers tinged with purple. Look for Canada violet in aspen groves that skirt the eastern edge of the park.

GOLDEN SEDGE
Carex aurea
Sedge Family (Cyperaceae)

Description: Golden sedge is a low, delicate perennial with a loosely tufted growth form. Its stems may reach 4 inches. Grass-like leaves about ¼ inch wide grow from the base of the plant. Flowers are unisexual (there are separate male and female flowers) and clustered into 2–5 well-separated spikes per flowering stem. Each spike is ¼–¾ inch long. The male spike is slender, brown in color and lies above the female spikes. Female flowers are composed of tiny, inflated, sac-like perigynia that are light green when young and golden brown at maturity. Clusters of female flowers are loosely grouped into grape-like clusters.

Habitat: Moist sites along wetlands and waterways from the montane zone to just above treeline.

Notes: The golden, grape-like clusters of golden sedge are its most distinctive characteristic. The plant is inconspicuous due to its low growth form, but its charming appearance makes it a delight to find growing among taller vegetation.

YELLOW SEDGE
Carex flava
Sedge Family (Cyperaceae)

Description: Yellow sedge is a tufted perennial with stems growing 4–20 inches tall. Its leaves are long, linear and resemble grass leaves. Flowers are unisexual (there are separate male and female flowers) and clustered into separate spikes at the stem top. All flowers lack true petals and sepals. Male flowers are small and arranged into a slender, brownish spike. Several globose female spikes lie below the male spike. Female flowers each have a yellowish, oval perigynium just under ¼ inch long with a pointed, reflexed beak. Clusters of perigynia radiate outward, giving each female spike a burr-like appearance.

Habitat: Common in wet soil of mountain meadows and wetlands and on streambanks; often found in sites with gravelly, calcareous soil.

Notes: Sedges are often overlooked when examining Glacier's flora, primarily due to their inconspicuous nature. With roughly 80 sedge (*Carex*) species in Glacier National Park, this group deserves recognition. Sedges resemble grasses, but have a distinctly different flower structure. Most notable is the presence of perigynia- inflated, egg-shaped sacs that enclose the ovary of female flowers.

ELK SEDGE
Carex geyeri
Sedge Family (Cyperaceae)

Description: Elk sedge is a loosely tufted, grass-like perennial growing 6–20 inches tall. Its leaves are long, linear and slightly stiff. Flowers are unisexual (there are separate male and female flowers). Lacking true petals and sepals, both types of flowers are clustered into a spike at the stem tip. Male flowers each have 3 protruding stamens and are tightly grouped at the top of each spike. Female flowers have a large ovary that is enclosed in a sac-like perigynium and has 3 styles at the tip. The perigynia are green, just under ¼ inch long, distinctly thumb-shaped with a rounded tip and subtended by a small, narrow, leaf-like bract. Bracts are just longer than the perigynia, sharp-pointed and brown with a pale midrib and margins. The few female flowers lie just below the cluster of male flowers.

Habitat: Common in well-drained soil of mountain grasslands, shrublands and open forests to the upper subalpine zone.

Notes: The tufted growth form, terminal male flower cluster and lower cluster of 1–3 perigynia are characters that help separate elk sedge from roughly 80 species of sedge (*Carex* species) that grow in Glacier National Park. Elk sedge is one of the most common sedges in montane and subalpine forests.

LAKESIDE SEDGE
Carex lenticularis
Sedge Family (Cyperaceae)

Description: Lakeside sedge is a tussock-form-ing perennial with erect to lax stems growing 6–32 inches tall. Its leaves are thin and grass-like. Flowers are tightly clustered into 3–6 long, slen-der spikes on short stalks at the stem tops. Each spike is ½–1¼ inches long and cylindrical with a thin, basal stalk. Male and female flowers are usually borne on separate spikes, with male spikes above. Female flowers form tiny, green, lens-shaped perigynia, each subtended by a small, dark bract (scale) with a pale midrib.

Habitat: Open habitats with saturated soil and/or standing water at all elevations; often occurs in wet meadows or along streams and lake shores.

Notes: Also known as lens-shaped sedge, this plant is one of Glacier's most abundant wet-site sedges. Its appearance is distinct. Water sedge (*C. aquatilis*) resembles lens-shaped sedge and grows in similar habitats, but its stems arise along spreading rhi-zomes and do not form tussocks.

MERTEN'S SEDGE
Carex mertensii
Sedge Family (Cyperaceae)

Description: Merten's sedge has a loosely tufted growth form and spreads via hori-zontal underground stems. The leaves are grass-like and roughly ¼ inch wide, and the stems grow 15–40 inches high. Flow-ers are tightly clustered into long-stalked, cylindrical spikes that dangle from the top of the main stem. Each spike is ½–1½ inches long and has unisexual flowers, with male flowers clustered below female flowers. In fruit, female flowers produce tiny, flattened, green to tan perigynia. They are elliptic and have a terminal beak. Each perigynium is subtended by a small, dark bract (scale) with a pale midrib.

Habitat: Widespread but never abundant in moist soil of shrub thickets and open forest in the montane and lower subalpine zones; often occurs along streams or lakes, and in drainage ditches along roads.

Notes: With its robust, elegant growth form and nodding spikes, Merten's sedge is one of Glacier's most beautiful sedge species. These characters also make it one of the easiest to identify.

SMALL-WINGED SEDGE
Carex microptera
Sedge Family (Cyperaceae)

Description: The stems and leaves of small-winged sedge form tussocks 8–32 inches tall. The leaves are grass-like, very thin and all on the lower half of the stem. Bisexual spikes (both male and female flowers on 1 spike) are tightly clustered into a globe-shaped head ½–1 inch long. Male flowers lie below female flowers on each spike. Flowers mature into green to light brown perigynia that are less than ¼ inch long and oval in outline with a tapered beak.

Habitat: Common in moist soil along streams, ponds and lakes and in moist meadows and grasslands; montane zone to treeline.

Notes: Small-winged sedge is closely related to several other sedge species that are common in Glacier National Park. A technical plant key is usually necessary to make a confident identification.

STALKED SEDGE
Carex podocarpa
Sedge Family (Cyperaceae)

Description: Stalked sedge is a loosely tufted perennial with spreading rhizomes. Its stems are 6–20 inches high. Leaves occur at the base and on the lower stem and are linear and grass-like. Flowers are tightly clustered into unisexual spikes (male spikes contain only male flowers; female spikes contain only female flowers) ½–¾ inch long. The uppermost spike is composed of male flowers, while the lower 2–4 are female and often nod on slender stalks. Female flowers produce dark purplish brown perigynia in fruit. Perigynia are tiny, flattened and narrowly oval in outline. They contain a single seed (achene). A small, dark scale subtends each perigynium.

Habitat: Abundant in wet to moist subalpine and alpine meadows; especially common near streams.

Notes: Stalked sedge is one of the most abundant high-elevation sedges in Glacier National Park. Look for it along the trail from Logan Pass to the Hidden Lake overlook. The alpine and subalpine habitats favored by stalked sedge are very fragile, so please tread lightly in these areas.

BEAKED SEDGE
Carex utriculata
Sedge Family (Cyperaceae)

Description: The stems of beaked sedge grow 20–40 inches tall and are 3-angled in cross section. They spread by sending shallow rhizomes under the soil surface and sometimes form dense thickets of plants. Leaves are long, grass-like and about ¼ inch wide. Flowers are tightly clustered into unisexual spikes (male spikes contain only male flowers; female spikes contain only female flowers). A slender group of 2–4 male spikes are produced above 2–5 female spikes. Female spikes are cylindrical, 1–3 inches long and well separated from the male spikes. They are subtended by leaf-like bracts. Perigynia are about ¼ inch long, oval in outline and tan with a stout beak.

Habitat: Abundant in saturated soil and standing water along streams, ponds, marshes and other wet areas; montane to lower subalpine zones.

Notes: Beaked sedge is the most common wet-area sedge in Glacier National Park. The female spikes resemble a bottlebrush. Look for the plant around almost any wet feature where sedges and willows grow. Beaked sedge was formerly called *C. rostrata*. That name now applies to a rare sedge that closely resembles beaked sedge, but has thinner leaves and a stem that is round in cross section.

CREEPING SPIKERUSH
Eleocharis palustris
Sedge Family (Cyperaceae)

Description: Creeping spikerush is a rhizomatous perennial forming sod of round stems 4–28 inches tall. Stems have a purple tinge at the base. Leaves are reduced to bladeless sheaths around the base of the stem. Flowers are densely clustered into a spike at the top of the stem. Spikes are egg- to lance-shaped, brownish and ¼–¾ inch long. Each flower consists of an ovary with 2–3 stigmas and 1–3 stamens and is subtended by a small brown scale. Ovaries mature into yellowish brown seeds (achenes). They are tiny and 2-sided with a conical projection at the top. Four barbed bristles, each just under ¼ inch long, extend from the achene base toward the top.

Habitat: Common in shallow, standing water and in wet soil in the montane zone; also occurs in soil that is wet only part of the growing season.

Notes: Creeping spikerush is Glacier's most common and conspicuous spikerush; there are 3 other species of spikerush in the park. Mature fruit and a technical plant key are necessary for positive identification of most of these plants.

TALL COTTONGRASS
Eriophorum polystachion
Sedge Family (Cyperaceae)

Description: Tall cottongrass is a rhizomatous perennial with stems growing 6–20 inches tall. Its leaves are grass-like and less than ¼ inch wide. Flowers are spirally arranged into 2–5 stalked spikelets that nod from the stem tip. Silky, white bristles 1–1½ inches long are produced when this plant is in fruit, forming cottony tufts. Fruits are dark, 3-sided achenes less than ¼ inch long. The spikelet cluster is subtended by 2–3 leaf-like bracts. Tall cottongrass forms its distinctive fluffy heads in late July and August.

Habitat: Forms colonies in moist to wet soil of mountain fens.

Notes: The downy, cotton-like spikelets make tall cottongrass an interesting and beautiful plant to behold, especially when it occurs over large areas. The equally common russet cottongrass (*E. chamissonis*) has a single spikelet at the stem tip with brownish bristles. Both species occupy similar habitats.

DRUMMOND'S RUSH
Juncus drummondii
Rush Family (Juncaceae)

Description: Drummond's rush is a slender, tussock-forming perennial with stiff, erect, leafless stems 4–12 inches tall. Flowers are borne singly or in a cluster of 2–5 that appears to protrude from the side of the stem. Each flower has 6 scale-like petals (tepals), each about ¼ inch long. They are brown with a green center and taper to a long point at the tip. In fruit, egg-shaped capsules are formed that split into 3 sections to release tiny, black seeds. Mature capsules are produced in July to September.

Habitat: Abundant in alpine meadows and turf, subalpine woodlands and shrublands. Most common in areas where snow lies late in the season.

Notes: The seeds of Drummond's rush have 2 slender tails, one on either end. A hand lens is usually necessary to observe this tiny detail.

SLENDER-STEMMED RUSH
Juncus mertensianus
Rush Family (Juncaceae)

Description: Slender-stemmed rush forms small tussocks connected by spreading rhizomes. Stems are 4–12 inches tall. Its leaves grow in an alternate pattern along the stem and are hollow, like a slender straw. A dense, globe-shaped cluster of brownish flowers is produced at the top of the stem. The flowers have 6 narrow, petal-like tepals, each less than ¼ inch long. In late summer an oblong capsule forms, splitting into 2 sections to release tiny, black seeds.

Habitat: Abundant in wet soil of alpine and subalpine meadows and along streams and ponds; occurs at lower elevations but is less common.

Notes: The dark, globose flower clusters (heads) of slender-stemmed rush are its most distinguishing feature. Look for this plant along small streams near Logan Pass. It can sometimes be seen growing in the ditches along Going-to-the-Sun Road near Lake McDonald.

HITCHCOCK'S WOOD RUSH
Luzula hitchcockii
Rush Family (Juncaceae)

Description: Hitchcock's wood rush is a low-growing, grass-like perennial that spreads by creeping rhizomes. Stems grow 4–12 inches tall. Leaves are linear and about ¼ inch wide, usually turning honey-colored soon after they emerge. Loosely branched clusters of brownish flowers are produced at the top of the stem. These clusters nod slightly on lax stalks. The ends of branches bear 1–2 flowers, each with 6 brown, scale-like, pointed petals (tepals). A central capsule is produced, slightly longer than the tepals, when this plant sets fruit. Capsules split into 3 parts to release many tiny seeds.

Habitat: Widespread in subalpine meadows, shrublands and forests; often occurs with beargrass (pg. 82) and common huckleberry (pg. 164).

Notes: What appear to be the petals of wood rushes (*Luzula* species) and rushes (*Juncus* species) are referred to as tepals, a term used when the sepals and petals of a flower look exactly alike. Piper's wood rush (*L. piperi*) and small-flowered wood rush (*L. parviflora*) are similar and occur in similar habitats, but both have smaller flowers.

MOUNTAIN BROME
Bromus carinatus
Grass Family (Poaceae)

Description: Mountain brome is a tussock-forming perennial with stems 2–3 feet high. It has a tiny ligule and its leaf blades are less than ½ inch wide. The leaf sheath is closed nearly to the top and covered with fine hair. Spikelets are ¾–1½ inches long, slightly flattened and arranged in a narrow, erect cluster at the stem top. Each individual flower has a short, needle-like awn. Mountain brome spikelets mature in July and August.

Habitat: Abundant east of the Continental Divide in grasslands, meadows, shrublands and woodlands, especially under aspen; less abundant in similar habitats west of the Divide; montane to lower subalpine zones.

Notes: Ongoing revegetation projects in Glacier National Park use mountain brome seed and nursery-grown seedlings for rehabilitation of disturbed sites. Smooth brome (*B. inermis*) and northern brome (*B. pumpellianus*) are similar perennial brome grasses, but they arise from horizontal underground stems (rhizomes) and do not form tussocks. Smooth brome is not native and is most common along roads; northern brome is native to North America and is common in grasslands on the east side of the park.

BLUEJOINT REEDGRASS
Calamagrostis canadensis
Grass Family (Poaceae)

Description: Bluejoint reedgrass is a robust perennial with stems 2–3 feet tall clustered along spreading rhizomes (underground stems). Its ligules are about ½ inch long and have a ragged edge. Leaves are roughly ½ inch wide. Spikelets are 1-flowered and arranged in a pyramid-shaped, branched inflorescence at the stem top. The outside of the spikelets often have a purplish tinge. The flowers have a tiny awn attached near the middle of the back and a tuft of white hair (callus hair) at the base. The callus hairs are almost as long as the flower. Bluejoint produces mature spikelets in July and August.

Habitat: Abundant in moist soil of wet meadows, seeps and in forest openings; often occurs around shallow ponds and streams; sometimes forms tall, dense mats of plants; montane to lower subalpine.

Notes: Purple reedgrass (*C. purpurascens*) also occurs in Glacier National Park, but is not as abundant as bluejoint reedgrass. Purple reedgrass has a narrow inflorescence and forms small tussocks without underground stems. It prefers drier, rockier habitats than bluejoint reedgrass.

PINEGRASS
Calamagrostis rubescens
Grass Family (Poaceae)

Description: Pinegrass is a delicate, slender plant with small tufts of stems 20–32 inches tall growing along rhizomes. Its ligules may be almost ¼ inch long, but are often smaller. Leaves are flat and less than ¼ inch wide. The leaf sheath is open and distinctively hairy at the top, forming a fluffy collar around the stem. Spikelets are arranged in a narrowly arrow-shaped inflorescence. The individual flowers have a needle-like awn projecting upward from the back. The awn is bent and extends out from the flower. Pinegrass blooms infrequently, in August.

Habitat: Abundant in dry mountain forests, often forming loose, wispy mats.

Notes: A sure-fire way to identify this plant is to look for the fluffy collar at the top of the leaf sheath. These plants often flower after a ground fire has moved through the forest understory. It's most commonly observed without flowers or flowering stems in the understory of a lodgepole pine forest.

SMOOTH WILDRYE
Elymus glaucus
Grass Family (Poaceae)

Description: Smooth wildrye is a tufted perennial with stems 1–3 feet high. Its broad leaves are flat, lax and ¼–½ inch wide. The leaf sheath is open and ligule is very small. Several (3–5) flowers are crowded into stalkless spikelets that overlap each other in a stiff, narrow spike at the stem top. The spike is about ½ inch long. Flowers are just under ½ inch long and usually have a needle-like awn ½–¾ inch long projecting from the tip. Smooth wildrye matures in June to September.

Habitat: Widespread in moist mountain forests, avalanche chutes, grasslands and meadows.

Notes: Smooth wildrye is one of the most abundant native grasses in Glacier National Park. It is similar to bluebunch wheatgrass (below), but has thicker flower heads and occurs in moister or shadier habitats. Native Americans used the grain of this plant for food.

BLUEBUNCH WHEATGRASS
Elymus spicatus
Grass Family (Poaceae)

Description: Bluebunch wheatgrass is a perennial grass forming tussocks with stems growing 1–3 feet high. Its leaves are very narrow and often inrolled along the edge. They are stiffly held at an upward angle from the stem. Several (6–8) flowers are tightly clustered into spikelets that barely overlap each other along a terminal spike. Each flower bears a long, bent, needle-like awn at the tip. Bluebunch wheatgrass spikelets mature in June to August.

Habitat: Abundant in mountain grasslands; common on sparsely vegetated slopes and ridges at higher elevations.

Notes: An unawned form of bluebunch wheatgrass occurs in the St. Mary Valley. This plant gets its common name from the bluish tinge it casts in grasslands where it dominates. It is also known as *Agropyron spicatum*.

ROUGH FESCUE
Festuca scabrella
Grass Family (Poaceae)

Description: Rough fescue is a tussock-forming perennial with stems 1–3 feet tall. Tussocks are dense and often as big around as a basketball. They are composed of new leaves as well as dried leaves from previous seasons. Leaves are narrow, rough to the touch and usually inrolled. They primarily arise from the plant base, but a few may be scattered along the flowering stem. Several tiny flowers are clustered into spikelets arranged at the tips of spreading to ascending branches. Mature spikelets form in June and July.

Habitat: Abundant in mountain and valley grasslands.

Notes: Rough fescue is the dominant grass in Glacier National Park's montane grasslands. The broad valley of the North Fork Flathead River is a perfect place to see rough fescue grasslands in relatively pristine condition. Idaho fescue (*F. idahoensis*, inset) is also abundant in the park and grows in similar habitats. It is much less robust than rough fescue, forming small tufts of slender leaves.

ALPINE TIMOTHY
Phleum alpinum
Grass Family (Poaceae)

Description: Alpine timothy forms small tussocks with stems up to 16 inches tall. Leaves are flat, about ¼ inch wide and rough-feeling along the margins. The leaf sheath is open where it wraps around the stem. One-flowered spikelets are arranged in tight, cylindrical clusters ½–1¼ inches long and just under ½ inch wide. Alpine timothy matures in July and August.

Habitat: Abundant in moist meadows, grasslands and on stony slopes from subalpine to alpine.

Notes: Alpine timothy establishes easily in recently disturbed soil. This characteristic has made it useful for revegetation projects in upper elevations. Look for it around the Logan Pass Visitor Center. An introduced, weedy relative, common timothy (*P. pratense*, inset), is usually a much larger plant and occurs at lower elevations. It is well established in some grasslands and along trails due to its introduction as forage for pack animals in the park's early years.

ALPINE BLUEGRASS
Poa alpina
Grass Family (Poaceae)

Description: Alpine bluegrass is a tufted, native perennial with stems 2–12 inches tall, sometimes forming loose mats of plants. Leaves are mainly basal, less than ¼ inch long and have a distinctive prow-like tip. A pyramidal inflorescence at the stem top is composed of purplish brown spikelets at the ends of spreading branches. Each spikelet is about ¼ inch long, slightly flattened and contains several tiny flowers. Alpine bluegrass matures in June to August.

Habitat: Abundant in moist to dry, open sites from subalpine to alpine; less common lower.

Notes: Kentucky bluegrass (*P. pratensis*, inset), a troublesome, introduced relative of alpine bluegrass, is also common in Glacier National Park. It is a sod-forming, aggressive species commonly used in lawns. Its spread is relatively limited to developed areas and along trails at lower elevations in the park.

DOWNY OATGRASS
Trisetum spicatum
Grass Family (Poaceae)

Description: Downy oatgrass is a tussock-forming perennial with stems 4–24 inches high. Its foliage is short-hairy below the inflorescence. Leaves are stiff, less than ¼ inch wide and may be flattened or slightly folded. Spikelets are clustered into a spike-like inflorescence 1–3 inches long at the stem top. Each spikelet contains 2 tiny flowers. The inflorescence may be purplish, greenish or brown. Spikelets mature in July and August.
Habitat: Abundant in moist to dry, rocky soil of open sites from subalpine to alpine.
Notes: The bent awns projecting outward from each spikelet are a distinctive characteristic of this grass. They give the flower clusters a bristly appearance, which is helpful in making a positive identification. Downy oatgrass, like many high-elevation grasses, provides important forage for the bighorn sheep, mountain goats and deer that range in subalpine and alpine habitats.

GLOSSARY

Achene. A small, dry, seed-like fruit that encloses a single seed.

Alpine. Refers to an altitudinal level where trees are no longer able to successfully establish.

Alternate. A type of arrangement whereby an element such as a leaf occurs singly at each node along a stem or branch.

Annual. A plant that completes its life cycle (germinating, producing seeds for a new generation, then dying) within a single year.

Anther. A small, sac-like, pollen-bearing structure located at the tip of the stamen.

Appressed. Lying tightly pressed against another surface.

Aquatic. Living wholly or partially submerged in water.

Armed. Having sharp structures such as spines or thorns.

Ascending. Growing in an upward direction but not strictly erect.

Awn. A slender, stiff, bristle-like appendage adorning a structure.

Axil. The upper side of the joint between two structures such as a leaf and stem.

Banner. The upper petal of a flower in the pea family. Sometimes broad and flag-like.

Barb. A short, sharp, backward-facing thorn.

Basal. Positioned at the bottom or base.

Beak. A firm, slender, elongated appendage extending from a structure such as a seed.

Biennial. A plant that is strictly vegetative for one or more years, then blooms once and dies.

Bisexual. Possessing both male and female flowers or flower parts.

Blade. Portion of the leaf that is typically broad and flat. Attached to the stem by the petiole.

Bract. A reduced or modified leaf often closely associated with a flower or flower cluster.

Bulb. A thickened, underground bud surrounded by fleshy, sometimes leaf-like scales.

Calcareous. Rich in calcium. Often refers to soils derived from such parent material as limestone.

Callus. The stiff lower portion of a grass flower.

Calyx. The outermost series of flower parts; the collective sepals.

Canopy. The uppermost layer of branches and/or stems. Often used to describe the above-ground structure of a coniferous forest.

Capsule. A dry fruit that splits open at maturity to release seeds.

Catkin. A tight, elongated cluster of unisexual flowers lacking petals and sepals. Usually hanging in a downward, cascading arrangement.

Chlorophyll. Green plant pigment used in photosynthesis to convert water and carbon dioxide into sugars.

Clasping. Partially or completely surrounding a stem or branch. Often in reference to a leaf with a broad base, lacking a petiole.

Compound. Divided into smaller segments. Often in reference to leaves divided into leaflets or flower clusters divided into smaller clusters.

Cone. Reproductive structure of some non-flowering plants that contains seeds or pollen subtended by scale-like bracts. Usually cylindrical.

Congested. Crowded together.

Corolla. The collective petals of a flower, which may be separate from each other or united into a bowl- or tube-shaped structure.

Crown. The upper portion of a tree's leaves and branches, or the upper portion of plant roots, where they meet the stem.

Deciduous. Dropping or shedding at the end of the growing season. Usually descriptive of leaves.

Dioecious. Having only male flowers or female flowers.

Disk flower. A tubular flower produced by a plant in the Sunflower Family (Asteraceae).

Dissected. Deeply divided into many lobes or segments.

Disturbed. Altered by activities that remove some existing vegetation, such as grazing or plowing.

Drupe. A fruit with a single seed that is enclosed in a stony covering and surrounded by a fleshy exterior (e.g., a cherry or peach).

Elliptic. Oblong or oval in outline, with rounded ends and a wide midsection.

Entire. Smooth along the edge, without teeth or lobes. Often descriptive of leaf margins.

Erect. Strictly upright.

Evergreen. Having foliage that stays green through at least one winter.

Fen. Mineral-rich wetland characterized by organic soil, usually dominated by sedges and mosses.

Fleshy. Referring to tissue that is plump and succulent.

Floodplain. Landform built by deposition of stream gravels through repeated flooding.

Floret. A tiny flower of the Grass (Poaceae) family.

Flower head. Tight cluster of tiny, unstalked flowers arranged on a hemispheric flowering structure.

Forb. A non-woody, broad-leaved herbaceous plant.

Frond. The leaf of a fern, often divided into segments.

Fruit. A mature ovary, complete with any covering tissue that may be present upon ripening.

Generic name. The scientific name for a group of plants that are related at the taxonomic level of genus.

Genus. A group of plant species that are closely related to each other. A genus may have only one member species.

Gland. A tiny organ that discharges sticky or oily fluid, often appearing like a small colored knob.

Glandular. Gland-bearing.

Glandular-hairy. Bearing hair tipped with tiny glands.

Herb. A plant with non-woody stems and branches that dies back to the ground after each growing season.

Herbaceous. Referring to vegetation that is non-woody.

Herbage. Aboveground, vegetative portion of a plant consisting of leaves and stems.

Hybrid. Offspring produced by parents of genetically different species.

Indusium, pl. **indusia.** Membranous covering that shelters spore clusters on the underside of a fern leaf.

Inflorescence. The flower cluster or flower arrangement of a plant.

Insectivorous. Having the ability to digest insects.

Introduced. Brought to one continent from another.

Involucral bracts. Small, scale-like leaves forming a cup-like structure around a cluster of flowers.

Keel. A prominent ridge that lies along a joint or fold, as in the keel of a boat. Often refers to the joined lower petals of flowers in the Pea family (Fabaceae).

Krummholz. A stunted, shrub-like growth form characteristic of trees growing at treeline, caused by windblown snow and exposure to very cold temperatures.

Lateral. On or toward the side.

Latex. Rubber-containing compounds in milky sap produced by some plants.

Leaf axil. The upper side of the joint between a leaf and stem.

Leaflet. Leaf-like subunit of a larger, compound leaf.

Lemma. The lower and outermost of two scale-like bracts that enclose a single grass flower.

Ligule. Short projection at the top of a grass or sedge leaf sheath, where the sheath meets the leaf blade. Often membranous or hairy.

Linear. Narrow and line-shaped, with essentially two parallel sides.

Lobe. Round or sharp projection that stands out from the margin of a leaf, petal or fruit.

Longitudinal. Aligned with the long axis.

Margin. Outside edge.

Marsh. Wetland characterized by nutrient-rich mineral soil, standing or slow-moving water and non-woody vegetation.

Membranous. Referring to tissue that is thin and pliable.

Mesic. Characterized by moderate moisture; mesic sites are ideal for plant growth.

Midrib. Central vein of a structure such as a leaf or bract. Sometimes elevated.

Node. A point along a stem where branches or leaves attach.

Nutlet. A tiny, hard, thick-walled fruit bearing a single seed.

Oblong. Narrowly elliptic but wider toward the tip than the base.

Opposite. Directly across from each other. A description of the placement of leaves along a stem.

Ovary. Female flower structure that contains developing seeds.

Ovate. Oval, but with one end slightly wider than the other. Egg-shaped in outline.

Palmate. Referring to the arrangement of leaflets on a petiole in which all leaflet bases attach to a single point; resembles the arrangement of fingers on a hand.

Panicle. A loosely branched arrangement of flowers that starts blooming at the bottom.

Pappus. Fine bristles or scales attached to the top of fruit in the Sunflower Family (Asteraceae).

Parasitic. Drawing water and/or food from another organism (host) at the host's expense.

Parasitize. To enter into a parasitic relationship with a host organism.

Pemmican. A food historically prepared by Native Americans; a mixture of pounded and dried meat and berries.

Perennial. A plant that survives the winter, producing new leaves and flowers each growing season.

Perigynium, pl. perigynia. The sac-like flower structure enclosing a hard achene in the genus Carex.

Petal. One member of the corolla (the inner, typically colorful and showy series of flower parts).

Petiole. The stalk that attaches a leaf blade to the stem.

Photosynthesis. The process by which plants convert water, carbon dioxide and minerals into energy, using sunlight.

Pinnate. Referring to an arrangement of leaflets, lobes or other elements that are positioned opposite each other along a single axis.

Pod. A dry fruit that splits open at maturity to release seeds.

Pollen. Tiny, sperm containing particles produced by male reproductive structures (anthers).

Pome. A fleshy fruit with a central, multi-chambered core (e.g., an apple)

Prostrate. Lying on or growing along the ground.

Raceme. A spike-like cluster of stalked flowers that begins blooming at the bottom.

Ray flower. A flower of the Sunflower family with a strap-shaped corolla, often positioned around the perimeter of the flower head.

Rhizomatous. Able to produce rhizomes.

Rhizome. An underground stem (often horizontal) with nodes or buds that may sprout above ground.

Riparian. Associated with a river.

Rosette. A cluster of basal leaves arranged in a circle, radiating outward from a central point.

Rootcrown. An underground, often thickened portion of stem growing from the top of the root(s).

Runner. A slender, above-ground horizontal stem that may root at the nodes.

Scale. A small, thin, often leaf-shaped structure.

Scree. A collection of rocky, sandy debris. Often occurs on slopes below crumbling rock walls.

Sedge. A member of the Sedge Family (Cyperaceae), with a grass-like growth form.

Sepal. An individual part of the collective calyx, the outer series of flower parts. Usually green, but may be colorful and showy in some species.

Serotinous. Delayed, as in delayed opening of flowers or cones. Often refers to cones that stay closed for years until high temperatures cause them to open.

Sheath. A structure that completely surrounds another structure, for example a grass-leaf sheath that surrounds a stem.

Shrub. A plant characterized by woody stems.

Species. A collection of closely related organisms that are capable of interbreeding and share many discerning characteristics.

Spike. A slender inflorescence with flowers attached directly to an axis.

Spikelet. A small spike, sometimes secondary. Often occurring in the Grass and Sedge families.

Sporangiophore. Leaf-like structure bearing sporangia.

Sporangium, pl. **sporangia.** A spore-containing structure.

Spore. A tiny, single-celled reproductive structure capable of yielding a new individual.

Sporophyll. A leaf that bears spores. Produced in non-flowering plants such as ferns.

Spur. A long, hollow appendage projecting from a petal or sepal. Often nectar bearing toward the base.

Stamen. The male portion of a flower, composed of an anther and a filament.

Sterile. Non-reproductive; vegetative only.

Stigma. The portion of the female reproductive organ (pistil) that receives pollen.

Stipule. An appendage growing at the junction between the leaf and stem.

Stolon. A horizontal, above-ground stem that may root at nodes, producing roots and shoots; a runner.

Stomate, pl. **stomata.** A tiny opening on a leaf surface through which air passes.

Style. The long, thin, tubular portion of a female reproductive organ (pistil) between stigma and ovary.

Subtend. To lie just underneath.

Succulent. Refers to tissue that is fleshy, juicy and somewhat thickened.

Talus. A collection of loose, unstable, rocky debris. Typically deposited on a steep slope below a rock wall.

Taproot. The principal descending root produced by some plants.

Tendril. A thin, curling strand growing from the end of a leaf or branch that enables some plants to climb.

Tepal. Refers to either a petal or a sepal when the two are indistinguishable.

Terminal. The outermost or uppermost point.

Treeline. The upper elevational limit of successful tree establishment.

Tundra. Low-growing vegetation that forms in high-elevation sites above treeline, typically dominated by sedges and/or small broad-leaved plants.

Turf. Dense, low-growing vegetation that often forms in moist sites at high elevation. Typically dominated by grasses and grass-like plants.

Tussock. A dense hummock formed by compressed growth of plant stems and leaves.

Umbel. A flower arrangement formed by pedicels that originate from a single point on the stem or branch tip, forming a somewhat flat-topped or umbrella-shaped flower cluster.

Unisexual. Comprised of a single sex, either male or female.

Vein. A small, tubular structure responsible for transporting water and/or nutrients. Often visible in the leaf blade of a plant.

Weed. A plant that grows plentifully in an undesirable location, displacing native vegetation. In North America most weeds are of European origin.

Whorl. A collection of 3 or more structures (e.g., leaves or branches) attached in a ring around a stem or branch.

Wing. A thin, flat extension protruding from the tip or side of a structure. In the Pea family (Fabaceae), the 2 side flower petals are wings.

SELECTED REFERENCES

Coombes, Allen J. *Dictionary of Plant Names.* Portland, OR: Timber Press, 1985.

Dorn, Robert D. *Vascular Plants of Montana.* Cheyenne: Mountain West Publishing, 1984.

Kershaw, Linda, Andy MacKinnon and Jim Pojar. *Plants of the Rocky Mountains.* Renton, WA: Lone Pine Publishing, 1998.

Kershaw, Linda. *Edible and Medicinal Plants of the Rockies.* Renton, WA: Lone Pine Publishing, 2000.

Lesica, Peter. *Flora of Glacier National Park.* Corvallis: Oregon State University Press, 2002.

Martin, Alexander C., Herbert S. Zim and Arnold L. Nelson. *American Wildlife and Plants: A Guide to Wildlife Food Habits.* New York: Dover Publications, 1951.

Muenscher, Walter Conrad. *Poisonous Plants of the United States.* New York: Macmillan, 1939.

Phillips, H. Wayne. *Northern Rocky Mountain Wildflowers.* Helena: Falcon Publishing, 2001.

Plowden, C. Chicheley. *A Manual of Plant Names,* 2nd ed. New York: Philosophical Library, 1970.

Schreier, Carl. *A Field Guide to Wildflowers of the Rocky Mountains.* Moose, WY: Homestead Publishing, 1996.

Shaw, Richard J. and Danny On. *Plants of Waterton-Glacier National Parks and the Northern Rockies.* Missoula, MT: Mountain Press, 1979.

Strickler, Dee. *Alpine Wildflowers.* Helena: Falcon Publishing, 1990.

Willard, Terry. *Edible and Medicinal Plants of the Rocky Mountains and Neighbouring Territories.* Alberta: Wild Rose College of Natural Healing, 1992.

INDEX

248

FOR MORE INFORMATION ABOUT GLACIER NATIONAL PARK

National Park Service
Glacier National Park
P.O. Box 128
West Glacier, Montana 59936
(406) 888-7800 (voice)
(406) 888-7896 (TDD)
http://www.nps.gov/glac/home.htm

Glacier Natural History Association
P.O. Box 310
West Glacier, MT 59936
Phone 406-888-5756
www.glacierassociation.org

The Glacier Natural History Association is the park's interpretive association and an excellent source for books, maps, and educational opportunities.

FOR MORE COPIES OF THIS BOOK

Please visit your local bookstore, contact the Glacier Natural History Association above, or contact:

Riverbend Publishing
PO Box 5833
Helena, MT 59604
Phone toll-free 1-866-787-2363
www.riverbendpublishing.com